**Enhancing equity through inquiry**

# Enhancing equity through inquiry

Lexie Grudnoff, Fiona Ell, Mavis Haigh,
Mary Hill, and Kīmai Tocker

In association with Carol Becroft, Hannah Cox, Clare Jackson, Julie Mana'o,
Frances Nelson, Rachel Oliver, Paula Passfield, Natasha Pritchard,
Greg Roebuck, Kusum Singh, and Marya Tanner

**NZCER PRESS**

NZCER PRESS
New Zealand Council for Educational Research
PO Box 3237
Wellington
New Zealand

www.nzcer.org.nz

© Authors, 2019

ISBN: 978-1-98-854262-1

No part of the publication (other than the worksheets and other student resources) may be copied, stored, or communicated in any form by any means (paper or digital), including recording or storing in an electronic retrieval system without the written permission of the publisher. Education institutions that hold a current licence with Copyright Licensing New Zealand may copy from this book in strict accordance with the terms of the CLNZ Licence.

A catalogue record for this book is available from the National Library of New Zealand.

Designed by Smartwork Creative Ltd

# Contents

| | |
|---|---|
| Acknowledgements | vii |
| Foreword | ix |
| **Chapter 1  Framing the project: Equality, equity, and inquiry for teaching** | **1** |
| Equity or equality? | 2 |
| Facets of Practice for Equity | 3 |
| Inquiry | 8 |
| Teacher inquiry and the Facets of Practice for Equity | 10 |
| Context | 11 |
| Summary | 11 |
| **Chapter 2  Building a strong Collaborative Inquiry Community** | **13** |
| What we did | 13 |
| What we learnt about building an effective, strong inquiry community | 17 |
| Creating collaborative communities | 22 |
| Learning about different forms of inquiry | 23 |
| Exploring and utilising evidence | 25 |
| Summary | 25 |
| **Chapter 3  Using the Facets of Practice for Equity to improve the teaching of mathematics** | **27** |
| Using the Facets of Practice for Equity to think differently | 29 |
| Using buddies to build communication in mathematics | 31 |
| Sharing evidence with learners | 34 |
| What can be learnt from our experience of using the Facets of Practice for Equity and Inquiry to tackle inequity in mathematics teaching and learning? | 37 |
| **Chapter 4  Enhancing equity through connecting to students as learners, and to their lives and experiences** | **39** |
| Taking stock of our partnership with students, families, and whānau | 40 |
| Investigating new approaches to homework | 43 |
| Findings from our inquiries | 47 |
| Conclusions | 49 |
| **Chapter 5  Cross-school collaborative inquiry to address school-wide problems of practice** | **51** |
| Finding out what was going on in our schools | 52 |
| What we learnt from undertaking inquiries as a cross-school CIT | 59 |

| Chapter 6 **Principals' perspectives on the project** | 61 |
|---|---|
| Creating connections to improve practice | 62 |
| Building capacity | 63 |
| Teacher inquiry and research | 64 |
| Concluding thoughts | 64 |
| Chapter 7 **Enhancing equity through inquiry: Key findings** | 66 |
| Collaborative inquiry for equity | 66 |
| Implications and possibilities for collaborative inquiry | 79 |
| References | 82 |
| **Index** | 86 |

## Figures

| | | |
|---|---|---|
| Figure 3.1: | The relationship between the elements of *what* (curriculum focus), *why* (Facets of Practice for Equity) and *how* (through inquiry) in developing the Collaborative Inquiry Team's focus | 28 |
| Figure 3.2: | Students working together to make shapes with pipe cleaners | 35 |
| Figure 4.1: | List of school–home connections prior to beginning the inquiry | 40 |
| Figure 4.2: | Homework survey for parents and whānau | 42 |
| Figure 4.3: | Example of a homework project | 44 |
| Figure 4.4: | Examples of student/parent collaborative projects from the senior syndicate | 45 |
| Figure 4.5: | Findings post-implementation of the new homework approaches | 46 |
| Figure 4.6: | Equality and equity | 49 |

## Tables

| | | |
|---|---|---|
| Table 5.1 | Summary of white-stick incidents over a 2-week period | 54 |
| Table 5.2 | Summary of incidents of challenging behaviour where children were sent to an SMT member over a 2-week period | 57 |
| Table 7.1 | Eight features of successful collaborative inquiry to increase equity | 67 |
| Table 7.2 | Facets of Practice for Equity | 78 |

## Acknowledgements

We are grateful for the funding we received from the Teaching and Learning Research Initiative (TLRI), which supported the project that gave rise to this book.

Thank you to everyone who participated in the project for your willingness and openness to inquire into your practice to benefit student learning and engagement.

We also thank Hilary van Uden for her careful copyediting of the manuscript.

# Foreword

*Marilyn Cochran-Smith*

Not long ago, I marked my 40th year as a teacher educator, having supervised my first student teachers and taught my first teacher education courses in 1978 while still a doctoral student. Since then, I've worked continuously as a teacher education practitioner, researcher, and scholar at two urban-serving universities in the US—the University of Pennsylvania in Philadelphia and Boston College in Boston. Along the way, I've been lucky enough to be visiting scholar, adjunct faculty, or policy advisor at multiple sites from Seattle to Singapore, Dublin to Tel Aviv, Oslo to Auckland.

My favourite among all my rich national and international experiences has been my 12-year collaboration with a group of teacher education colleagues—who long ago became friends—at the Faculty of Education and Social Work at The University of Auckland. It is my association with these colleagues that connects me to this important book, for which I am honoured to write the foreword.

## *Situating this book*

As the two pieces of its title suggest, *Enhancing equity through inquiry* takes up two widely discussed issues in education research, practice, and policy. The first—promoting equity—has to do with efforts to (re)conceptualise and (re)organise schools and classrooms to ensure equitable opportunities and outcomes for students, families, and communities traditionally not well served by the system. The second—inquiry—has to do with efforts to position collaborative inquiry by teachers and other practitioners as a central aspect, not just of teacher learning, but of the broader transformation of teaching and learning in schools. Each of these issues has received national and international attention over the past several decades, as the many existing books on each topic attest.

There have also been multiple efforts to combine the two topics of equity and teacher inquiry, as this book does. This trend is evidenced by the many existing explorations of the role of teacher research and other forms of practitioner inquiry in enhancing marginalised students' learning opportunities and their life chances. In addition, much of the research about the processes and practices of preparing teachers for diversity in initial teacher education programmes has been conducted by teacher educators researching their own programmes, courses, fieldwork sites, and school collaborations using the data of practice and informed by a variety of diversity and equity-related conceptual frameworks. In a certain sense, then, *Enhancing equity through inquiry* is in good company. It joins a host of other books and articles about the promise—and, sometimes, the impact—of teacher inquiry in contributing to more equitable learning opportunities and outcomes for marginalised students, families, and communities.

It seems fair to ask, then, "What's so special about this book?" Plenty. In fact, *Enhancing equity through inquiry* is a deceptively small book with a big message. Below, I focus on two of the many things that make this slim volume important and powerful.

## *Enhancing equity/promoting inquiry*

This book takes us deep inside the work of a 2-year collaborative inquiry community committed to promoting equity within and across two Auckland primary schools that serve low-socioeconomic communities with large percentages of Māori and Pasifika students. The inquiry community was made up of nine teachers from the schools, the two principals, and five University of Auckland teacher educators who had long-standing relationships with those school communities. There were two within-school "Collaborative Inquiry Teams" (CITs), each made up of teachers and teacher educators, as well as one cross-school team comprised of deputy principals and a teacher educator. The teams also came together in a joint "Collaborative Inquiry Community" (CIC), which allowed for consideration of cross-school and cross-team issues. The inquiry community spent a full year exploring what it meant to teach for equity. They did so, as the early chapters of the book explain, using the "Facets of Practice for Equity" (Facets) framework, which several of the teacher educators had developed based on their analysis of relevant international research. (I say more about this framework in the next section.)

One important contribution of this book is that it reveals how the inquiry community worked during their first year. They did not simply "adopt" the Facets framework, nor did the teachers learn from the teacher educators how to "apply" the Facets to their work. Rather, with the CITs, everybody was assumed to be a "knower" as well as a learner and a teacher. Everybody had questions and uncertainties, including the principals. Over time, the group built a sense of trust in each other and a willingness to expose their own questions about practice as grist for their own and others' learning. Over time, raising questions and being uncertain about what it means to teach for equity came to be seen as a sign of learning, not a sign of failing. Over time and working together, the inquiry teams interrogated the Facets framework—clarifying, raising questions, and connecting the ideas represented by the Facets to concrete issues and practices in their classrooms and schools. But they also critiqued the Facets, identified omissions, elaborated concepts, and added meanings. In short, during that first year, the groups worked from an inquiry stance on teaching for equity wherein inquiry is regarded not as a project or set of steps to solve a problem, but as a perspective and a point of view about being a practitioner in a complex and changing world.

The chapters of the book focus on how the groups built on their understandings of teaching for equity during the second year of the project by taking up specific equity issues and topics in the schools. These chapters provide many rich and sensitive examples of classroom and school work that will be helpful to Aotearoa New Zealand teachers / teacher educators and to teachers / teacher educators in other countries and contexts. For example, through both words and evocative pictures, the chapter on children's mathematics learning includes multi-layered accounts of new entrant children, whose home language for many was not English, working with older children in tuakana–teina relationships. In this chapter, we see and read about groups of children making geometric shapes and measuring common objects while teachers and older buddies made videos or took photographs of the process. This allowed them to return to the activities in discussions that scaffolded mathematical talk for all the children, not just for those who already had confidence as speakers. The chapter on building partnerships with families also uses compelling pictures as well as words. Here we read about how both teachers' and families' attitudes and responses to homework changed over time, and we see vivid examples of children's creative and varied homework projects, which reflect the values, resources, and preferences of their families. The cross-school collaborative inquiry chapter illustrates how deputy principals and a teacher educator worked together to document incidences of challenging behaviours, and the contexts in which they occurred, across two schools where both practice and situations were different from one another.

Clearly this book provides examples of practitioners' ways of working for equity that others will find useful. Just as important are the specific questions the inquiry groups posed, during the second year of the project, based on their enhanced understandings of equity and their perspective on inquiry as a stance on practice. The mathematics chapter takes this up explicitly, pointing out that their group's conversations shifted from questions about what mathematics the children could or could not do to questions about how their own practices impacted children's access to mathematics learning, especially who did or did not have access. Similarly the partnership chapter suggests that instead of raising questions about how to get more children to complete homework, the inquiry community raised questions about how to build on the cultural, linguistic, and experiential resources of families to develop more appropriate expectations and approaches to homework in the first place. Another chapter, which is about challenging behaviour issues across the two schools, also reflects the synergy of enhanced ideas about equity coupled with an inquiry stance. The chapter explains that senior school leaders at both schools were concerned about increasing incidences of children exhibiting challenging behaviours. However, rather than jumping directly to new disciplinary practices and policies intended to reduce these behaviours, the inquiry team chose to begin by posing questions about what was actually happening at each school and gathering systematic evidence about the details of disciplinary instances. This allowed them to get beneath the surface of their own assumptions and get at the reasons behind the increases in challenging behaviours.

These new questions are consistent with the idea that practice is not simply what teachers or school leaders do at particular points in time. Rather it also involves how they think about what they do and the values, attitudes, and interpretive perspectives they use to make sense of what happens in the classroom, the school, and the community. The questions also reveal that teaching for equity is incredibly complex and multi-layered, which means that specific teaching actions cannot be fully determined and prescribed in advance of, or outside of, particular teaching and schooling contexts.

## *Research and practice, practice and research*

The second central contribution of this book is what it shows us about the relationship between educational research and practice. For many years there have been discussions about the problematic relationship of educational research and classroom/school-based practice, many of which have revolved around the idea that practitioners ought to pay more attention to research. This is reflected in complaints that teachers don't read research, they don't apply research to their practice, that teachers only care about what to do tomorrow, and that practice is based on fads and tradition instead of research-based evidence. On the other hand, there have also been recurring discussions that revolve around the idea that researchers ought to pay more attention to practice. This is reflected in complaints that research is irrelevant to practice, researchers are ignorant of the complexities of practice, research is too theoretical to be useful to practitioners, and research often yields nothing more than common sense that practitioners have known for years.

Even though both of these viewpoints are admittedly stated in the extreme, they are not completely far-fetched and are not simply ideas from the past. Indeed, we all hear complaints like these from time to time. This is the case even though the concepts of teacher research and practitioner inquiry have been around for decades, and they developed partly as a rejection of the assumption that research and practice inhabit two separate worlds, with research living primarily in the theoretical world of universities and practice living mostly in the practical world of schools.

The two-worlds fallacy does not make an appearance in *Enhancing equity through inquiry*. To the contrary, the book represents a fascinating and extended example of a mutual and synergistic relationship between research and practice that is akin to what we (Cochran-Smith & Lytle, 2009) have called "working the dialectic". I use the excerpt below to explain what this means and to show its clear affinity with the approach taken by the collaborative inquiry community that authored this book.

> The term dialectic refers to the tensions and presumed contradictions between a number of key ideas and issues that have to do with research, practice, and knowledge. The first, and perhaps most important of these, is the assumed dichotomy between research, on one hand, and practice, on the other; the second is the twin of the first—the assumed disjuncture between the role of the researcher and the role of the practitioner. When research and practice are assumed to be dichotomous, then analysis, inquiry and theorizing are understood to be part and parcel of the world of research, while action, experience and doing are considered integral to the world of practice.
>
> In contrast, practitioner research is defined, at least in part, by turning these dichotomies on their heads. With practitioner research, the borders between inquiry and practice are crossed, and the boundaries between being a researcher and being a practitioner are blurred. Instead of being regarded as oppositional constructs, then, inquiry and practice are assumed to be related to one another in terms of productive and generative tensions. From this perspective, inquiry and practice are understood to have a reciprocal, recursive, and symbiotic relationship, and it is assumed that it is not only possible, but indeed beneficial, to simultaneously take on the roles of both researcher and practitioner. This means that when university- or school-based educators "work the dialectic" of inquiry and practice, there are not distinct moments when they are only researchers or only practitioners. Rather these activities and roles are integrated and dynamic. (pp. 93–94)

Here is one way, then, to describe this book: *Enhancing equity through inquiry* is the story of a group of colleagues, some from a university and some from schools, all regarded as knowers and learners, who spent 2 years working the dialectic of research and practice towards the goal of promoting equity for high-priority students.

Images of what it really looks like to work the dialectic between research and practice are braided together throughout this book. To begin, a group of teacher educators, who were both practitioners and scholars, turned to research because they wanted to put equity at the centre of initial teacher education. They also wanted to study the conditions that supported teacher candidates' learning to teach for equity. They analysed international research syntheses to develop a set of "Facets of Practice for Equity" (Facets), which are described in detail in the book. They believed the Facets might also be useful to their colleagues in partner schools, where their candidates engaged in fieldwork and where some of the now-experienced teachers were their own former teacher candidates. But, as I noted above, they did not bring the Facets to the schools as research findings to be implemented. They brought them as principles and ideas to be questioned, explored, critiqued, and extended. This meant they spent a year working collaboratively with school-based teachers and principals to understand the Facets in the context of practice and, in the process, they became an inquiry community with enough trust to tackle hard questions. Their discussions led to the honing and clarification of some of the Facets, which became the centrepiece of an innovative initial teacher education programme, The University of Auckland's Master of Teaching (Primary) wherein teacher candidates engaged in teacher inquiry linking the Facets to their own emerging practice.

Meanwhile, the Collaborative Inquiry Community across two partner schools continued into its second year, engaging in the specific equity inquiries that are mentioned above and described in detail in the book. Here, as one of the chapters suggests, the Facets provided a "short list" of where to look for changes in practice that might increase equity. In essence, the Collaborative Inquiry Community and its multiple inquiry teams continuously worked the dialectic of research and practice, completely blurring the lines between their roles as researchers and practitioners.

*Enhancing equity through inquiry* is a unique book that offers compelling examples of inquiry for equity that will be useful locally and beyond. It is well worth the read.

Marilyn Cochran-Smith
*Cawthorne Professor of Teacher Education for Urban Schools*
*Lynch School of Education and Human Development, Boston College, Massachusetts*
*February 2019*

## Reference

Cochran-Smith, M., & Lytle, S. L. (2009). *Inquiry as stance: Practitioner research for the next generation.* New York, NY: Teachers College Press.

# Chapter 1
# Framing the project: Equality, equity, and inquiry for teaching

It is an unfortunate reality that over a number of years Aotearoa New Zealand's national and international achievement data show a large gap between our high-achieving and low-achieving learners. While other countries also have problems related to inequitable student outcomes, this problem takes on particular significance in Aotearoa New Zealand because of the relationship between achievement and students' ethnicity and socioeconomic background: Māori, Pasifika, and students from poor communities are persistently over-represented in the low-achieving group, while Pākehā (a New Zealander of European descent) and Asian students, often from better-off communities, are more likely to be found in the high-achieving group (Snook & O'Neill, 2014).

Despite numerous policy initiatives aimed at addressing our nation's achievement gap,[1] the evidence is clear that all of us in education continue to face a considerable challenge in knowing how to teach in ways that promote equitable learning outcomes and opportunities for

---

1 For example, the decade-old Ka Hikitia strategy has not been able to achieve the aim of changing how the education system serves Māori. Similarly, the Pasifika Education Plan, first introduced in 2001, has not reduced the disparities in achievement of Pasifika learners.

every student. This book seeks answers to a big question—what does it mean to teach for equity? Drawing on findings from the Teaching and Learning Research Initiative (TLRI)-funded project "Teaching for Equity: How Do We Do It?", this book aims to illustrate how educators can build shared understandings of teaching for equity and provides examples of what teaching for equity looks like in practice.

## *Equity or equality?*

In this book we use the term "equity" to show a commitment to justice and fairness based on the assumption that in Aotearoa New Zealand, as in many countries, educational opportunities, resources, and outcomes are not fairly distributed among groups differentiated by ethnicity, language, socioeconomic class, gender, or disability. We first need to define what we mean by equity, given that it is sometimes used as a synonym for equality.

The terms "equity" and "equality" are frequently used when policy makers talk about diverse students' learning opportunities and outcomes. This is certainly true in Aotearoa New Zealand policy reports and documents. For example, the Ministry of Education (2012) talks about the implementation of Treaty of Waitangi principles in delivering *The New Zealand Curriculum* in terms of the third principle, *participation*, relating to "an equality of opportunity and outcomes" (p. 4). The Education Review Office (ERO, 2016a) notes that the top challenge facing the Aotearoa New Zealand education system is to achieve equity and excellence in student outcomes.

While the terms "equity" and "equality" are similar and often used interchangeably, they do not mean the same thing. Equity means giving everyone what they need in order to be successful, which implies that some groups or individuals may require more than other groups or individuals. In contrast, equality is providing the same support for everyone. For equality to produce equal outcomes, everyone needs to start from the same place. The following two questions relating to school funding are intended to show the difference between the terms equality and equity. Question 1 asks "Should per-student funding at every school be exactly the same?" This is an equality question. Question 2 asks "Should students who come from less get more, to maximise their potential for success?" This is an equity question. The first question is principally about providing the same (an equal amount of) support to every learner, while the second question is principally to do with justice (providing enough support to achieve equitable outcomes for all learners).

While there has been a growing focus internationally on promoting teaching that enhances equitable outcomes for all learners, we are still struggling to find ways to address the ongoing problem of inequitable outcomes between advantaged and disadvantaged learners. Although we have valuable information about effective teaching strategies, variable student outcomes continue to present a challenge for all of us in education. Some scholars (e.g., Bishop & Berryman, 2006) have argued that to address this challenge we need to move away from focusing on discrete strategies or aspects of teaching and, instead, take a more holistic approach to teaching for equity. This belief led to the development of the "Facets of Practice for Equity" that, along with inquiry, framed the TLRI project that provided the basis for this book.

## *Facets of Practice for Equity*

Given that many countries face the problem of inequitable student outcomes, it is not surprising that a great deal of research has been undertaken to identify teaching practices that enhance diverse students' learning outcomes and opportunities. The TLRI project built on work undertaken by some of us as members of an international research group called Project RITE.[2] As part of Project RITE's research agenda, we explored what the international research said about teaching practices that have a positive effect on disadvantaged and other learners. The result of this conceptual analysis was the "Facets of Practice for Equity" (Facets), which underpinned our work as a collaborative inquiry community on what it means to teach for equity in Aotearoa

---

2   Rethinking Initial Teacher Education (RITE) is a two-country research team comprising researchers from Boston College, USA (Marilyn Cochran-Smith, Larry Ludlow) and The University of Auckland, New Zealand (Fiona Ell, Lexie Grudnoff, Mary Hill, Mavis Haigh). The fundamental premise underlying Project RITE is that the goal of initial teacher education is to prepare teachers who challenge inequities by enacting teaching practices that promote students' learning, broadly defined to include academic, social, emotional, civic, and critical learning.

New Zealand. Following is an overview of the two major tasks we undertook to develop the Facets.[3]

## Task 1: Identifying and selecting the research programmes/syntheses

Our first task comprised a search of major international programmes or syntheses of empirical research that met four major criteria:

1. The research took a complex view of teaching and learning.
2. Student outcomes were broadly conceived to include academic, social, emotional, civic, and critical learning.
3. The empirical evidence used to verify the practices could be traced and checked.
4. The identified practices had a positive impact on diverse learners.

It is important to note that we conceptualised teaching practices at the broad level of principles or themes rather than at the level of particular techniques or strategies.

As Project RITE has researchers from Aotearoa New Zealand and the United States, we were especially interested in drawing on research from these two countries. However, we also intentionally considered research undertaken in a range of countries because we wanted to see if, despite differences in political and policy contexts, we could identify similarities to inform our work. We eventually selected the following five research syntheses/large programmes of research that met the above criteria.

- Three research syntheses from the Best Evidence Synthesis programme (BES: Aotearoa New Zealand): Aitken and Sinnema, 2008; Alton-Lee, 2003; and Anthony and Walshaw, 2007. The BES programme, funded by the Ministry of Education, synthesises national and international empirical evidence about the impact of teaching practices for diverse learners. The findings from these three BES syntheses demonstrated links between teaching practices and student outcomes. They also identified

---

[3] See Grudnoff et al. (2017) for a detailed description of how the facets of practice for equity were developed.

teaching practices that were effective for diverse learners, although each synthesis classified these practices using different language. For example, *Quality Teaching for Diverse Students in Schooling* (Alton-Lee, 2003) produced 10 "research-based characteristics of quality teaching practices" (p. v); *Effective Pedagogy in Social Sciences* also identified quality teaching practices, calling them "mechanisms that facilitate learning" (Aitken & Sinnema, 2008, p. 52); and *Effective Pedagogy in Mathematics* (Anthony & Walshaw, 2007) established "key principles underpinning effective mathematics teaching" (p. 1). The findings from the BES syntheses have been widely used within Aotearoa New Zealand and have also informed curriculum and professional development programmes internationally.

- The Teaching and Learning Research Programme (TLRP: United Kingdom). The TLRP was a large-scale, government-funded programme of educational research on teaching and learning undertaken mainly between 2002 and 2009. The programme aimed to develop knowledge of how to improve outcomes (broadly defined) for all learners in all teaching and learning contexts. In contrast to the Aotearoa New Zealand BES, which brought together findings from previously published international research, the TLRP commissioned and co-ordinated around 700 researchers and 100 studies and projects on teaching and learning. Through a process of thematic analysis, the findings across these studies were synthesised into a set of 10 principles for effective learning and teaching (James & Pollard, 2011).

- The Measures of Effective Teaching project (MET: United States). The MET is a widely disseminated, large-scale 3-year project, established in 2009 and funded by the Bill and Melinda Gates Foundation. It aimed to build and test "fairly and reliably" (MET project, 2013, p. 3) measures of effective teaching that could be used to inform teachers about the skills that make them more effective. While the MET, with its focus on measuring practice, had a different aim from either Aotearoa New Zealand's BES or the United Kingdom's TLRP, its ultimate goal was also to improve student outcomes. The MET project, which focused on determining how to best identify and promote effective teaching, was a research partnership of academics, 3,000 teachers from seven public school districts, and education organisations. The MET project produced three major reports plus research papers and professional development material for teachers.

## Task 2: Comparing the research and developing the Facets

Our second major task was analysing each of the selected syntheses / programmes of research and then comparing and contrasting the results of these analyses. We were interested in seeing if there were commonalities across the findings from these different countries' research programmes in terms of teaching practice that has a positive influence on students' learning outcomes and opportunities. A number of the identified practices, such as providing a positive learning environment, are well known to teachers, researchers, and policy makers. What is noteworthy is that across these syntheses / programmes of research, which were very different in terms of context, scope, purpose, and methods, we were able to identify common themes about practice that are consistently associated with positive learning outcomes. We eventually developed five general principles, adjusted and readjusted through ongoing comparison, which we called "Facets of Practice for Equity".

The facets we originally developed through this process were:

**Facet 1** **Selecting worthwhile content and designing and implementing learning opportunities aligned to valued learning outcomes.** Examples of practice include teachers selecting and designing learning experiences that support students' understanding of content and conceptual development, and that enable students' active participation and achievement in learning.

**Facet 2** **Connecting to students' lives and experience.** In this facet, the focus is on teachers identifying and responding to students' prior knowledge, skills, interests, motivations, and level of engagement by making curriculum content relevant and inclusive to students' lives, languages, and cultures.

**Facet 3** **Creating learning-focused, respectful, and supportive learning environments.** Examples include teachers establishing cognitive, social, and emotional connections with students; recognising and valuing student diversity; and creating a sense of belonging to the class and school community.

**Facet 4** **Using evidence to scaffold learning and improve teaching.** Teachers use feedback processes from assessment to nurture students' learning, self-regulation, critical thinking, and metacognitive strategies. Teachers also use assessment evidence to adjust their teaching.

**Facet 5** **Adopting an inquiry stance and taking responsibility for further professional engagement and learning.** Here, teachers develop the knowledge and skills of inquiry in order to evaluate evidence, including evidence of learning. They develop the confidence to challenge, and inquire into, taken-for-granted assumptions, including their own. Teacher learning is both individual and collaborative.

As noted above, the MET project, the TLRP, and the BES programme were all undertaken because of a desire to address inequitable outcomes for diverse students in their countries of origin. The BES programme was especially interested in identifying practices shown to enhance the learning of Aotearoa New Zealand's most disadvantaged learners (Māori and Pasifika students). Given Project RITE's interest in teaching for equity, we also identified and analysed two additional frameworks that specifically focused on teaching practices shown empirically to enhance outcomes for historically disadvantaged students. From Aotearoa New Zealand we selected the government-funded Te Kotahitanga project, a programme of pedagogical and school reform begun in 2001 with the aim of improving outcomes for Māori students (Aotearoa New Zealand's indigenous population) who have been historically marginalised by the education system (Bishop, Berryman, & Wearmouth, 2014). From the United States we selected CREDE (Center for Research on Education, Diversity, and Excellence), which offers professional development to teachers of native Hawaiian descent and other diverse students. The original research on CREDE, begun in the 1970s, gave rise to principles that were effective for culturally and linguistically diverse students. These were developed into the CREDE Five Standards for Effective Pedagogy and Learning (Dalton, 2007).

Although both Te Kotahitanga and CREDE were smaller in scale and had a smaller number of standards or practices than our main data sources, the key findings from both aligned with the facets we had developed from the MET, TLRP, and BES. Te Kotahitanga and CREDE also highlighted the critical role that teachers play in improving disadvantaged students' opportunities by challenging inequities in terms of their own assumptions and practice. We therefore added a sixth facet to our initial list of five:

**Facet 6    Recognising and challenging classroom, school and societal practices that reproduce inequities.**

The evidence from the international programmes of research indicated that the six facets were sensitive to context (including classroom and school cultures) and to relationships with particular students and the resources they bring to school. In addition to being highly contextualised, the evidence suggested that the facets were also interconnected. Hence, because each facet is in relationship with other facets, we believe it would be difficult to enact one of these facets without enacting many of the others. For example, creating learning-focused, respectful, and supportive learning environments is facilitated through teachers connecting to students' lives and experiences. This, in turn, influences teachers' selection of worthwhile content and the design of learning opportunities. Similarly, in order to address equity, teachers should work from the assumption that the job of teaching involves enhancing students' learning opportunities and outcomes by recognising and challenging classroom, school, and societal practices that reproduce inequities. See Chapter 2, which describes how Facets 2 and 6 were changed through our work in the TLRI project.

## *Inquiry*

The second frame for the TLRI project that underpins this book was inquiry. *The New Zealand Curriculum* (Ministry of Education, 2007) (*NZC*) identifies *teaching as inquiry* as being a key part of how teachers ensure success for all the students in their class. The purpose of teaching as inquiry is for teachers to improve their practice by examining, through a cyclical inquiry process, the impact of their teaching on their students. However, inquiry as we use it in this book is broader than teaching as inquiry as outlined in *NZC* in two ways. First, we regard inquiry as being a matter of stance (Cochran-Smith & Lytle, 2009), a world view or a critical habit of mind, whereby teachers continually question how their practice impacts on children's learning but also ask wider questions about how differential educational resources, processes, and practices influence student outcomes. Secondly, we believe that *inquiry as stance* means drawing on the collective knowledge and wisdom of practitioners as being key to improving classroom and school inequities. Thus, inquiry as stance often involves teachers in collaborative inquiry processes.

In this project, we built on the evidence-based idea that teacher professional learning and students' learning are enhanced through teachers' engagement in collaborative inquiry communities. For example, Cochran-Smith and Lytle (2009) documented the international use of professional learning inquiry communities, which aimed to improve students' learning and enhance their life chances. They argued that when inquiry is taken up as a stance on teaching, learning, and schooling, inquiry communities generate local knowledge, re-envision and theorise their practice, and interpret and interrogate the theory and research of others. Similarly, Fullan (2011) identified the benefits of effective collaborative practice both in and between schools, as well as the need for well-led teams of teachers working together to build individual and collective capacity to improve student outcomes. He contended that while it might be "easier" to go to a professional development workshop or course, the learning that occurs at school with colleagues is much more powerful in terms of underpinning sustainable pedagogical change. The notion that collaborative practice within and across schools results in better learning for diverse students also aligns with policy initiatives such as the Ministry of Education's Teacher-led Innovation Fund (TLIF), which is designed to support quality practice that improves student achievement and can be shared and adapted for use across schools. The power of collaborative practice also underpins many of the recommendations in the report by the Tomorrow's Schools Independent Taskforce (Ministry of Education, 2018).

Engagement in collaborative inquiry communities, which is the focus of this book, can thus be viewed as professional learning that aims to change teachers' practice, transform classrooms, disrupt old habits, and alter mindsets. However, the outcomes of professional learning are rarely this radical, and change as a result of professional learning is often negligible or temporary (Opfer & Pedder, 2011; Timperley, Wilson, Barrar, & Fung, 2007). That is because professional learning, and the changes it promotes, are sometimes seen as "add-ons" by some teachers: just more things they have to do in addition to what they do at present. Too many add-ons result in stress and disillusionment, with teachers preferring to stick to what they know and do well, rather than take additional risks that are time-consuming and difficult. Teachers, however, can and do change their practice when they have a strong moral purpose for doing so (Timperley, Kaser, & Halbert, 2014).

Schools often select a focus for a year as an area upon which the whole school will work together. Sometimes it's a curriculum area, such as writing or physical education, and sometimes it's a broader issue such as positive behaviour management or engaging parents with the school. Focus areas may also arise through collaboration with other schools. The focus area, be it curriculum or wider concerns, provides the "what" of the inquiry: the area in which improvement is needed. There are a variety of approaches that schools take to tackling their focus area, but increasingly some form of teacher inquiry is being used. This may include learning with outside facilitators, or attending courses, conferences, or webinars, but it centres on defining a student learning issue, gathering information about the impact of current practice, trying something new, using evidence to evaluate whether or not it worked, and adapting practice in response to the evidence collected. Inquiry provides a "how" for professional learning, giving a method by which improvements can be made and evaluated.

## Teacher inquiry and the Facets of Practice for Equity

For classroom teachers, both the school focus and the inquiry process can seem like add-ons if they are not accompanied by an understanding of how these activities will help learners and tackle inequity in the school and classroom. The Facets outlined above bring to the fore the moral purpose of changing classroom practice. The Facets emphasise the capacity of teachers' practice to reduce inequity in the classroom and to speak back to inequity in broader social contexts. Rather than being an add-on to a professional learning focus, the Facets can be a driver for teachers' participation and change because they provide a "why" for the new learning and practice change in which teachers are being asked to engage. Although the Facets provide a broad description of teacher actions and orientations that improve equity (and thus could be seen as what to do and how to do it), in framing an inquiry they provide the reason why certain choices are made or directions taken. They give an answer to the commonly posed "so what?" question that can be asked after an inquiry process.

## *Context*

As noted above, this book seeks answers to a big question: What does it mean to teach for equity? To help us provide answers to this question, a collaborative inquiry community comprising nine Auckland primary teachers and five university researchers came together to generate and share knowledge about teaching for equity. The teachers were from two Auckland primary schools located in low-socioeconomic communities: New Lynn and Fairburn. The principals of both schools also participated in the project. Each school had approximately 15% Māori students. New Lynn had 31% Pasifika students and Fairburn had 47%. New Lynn had a high proportion of children with learning support needs. The teachers in both schools were culturally diverse. The teacher educators had long-established relationships with the schools, involving both initial teacher education and professional learning innovations. We all shared a strong moral purpose for being involved in the project—the desire to improve learning outcomes and opportunities for learners in Aotearoa New Zealand.

## *Summary*

This book aims to provide practical examples of what it means to teach for equity in Aotearoa New Zealand. We wanted to test the relevance and usefulness of the six Facets of Practice for Equity for Aotearoa New Zealand teachers, and show how a collaborative inquiry community can develop rich understandings of equitable teaching practices through engagement in robust and extended discussions. This is described in the next chapter, Chapter 2. We also wanted to develop in-depth examples of how teachers can use inquiry as a research process to identify and inquire into problems of practice and to improve ways they engage with and teach all learners in their classrooms and the wider school. These examples are described in the form of case studies in Chapters 3, 4, and 5.

# Chapter 2
# Building a strong Collaborative Inquiry Community

In Chapter 1 we explained why using the "Facets of Practice for Equity" (Grudnoff et al., 2017) and a process of inquiry could be an effective way to address inequity in schools. In this chapter we show how we built and worked within a strong collaborative inquiry community to explore notions of equity and practice for equity. We begin by giving some brief details about the project to make it clear where our ideas come from. We then address the importance of building strong and trusting relationships within the community, the significance of the Facets in providing a conceptual framework for the project, the creation of collaborative communities, and the importance of diversity in collaborative discussion. We finish with a discussion on different types of inquiry and the role of evidence in inquiry.

## *What we did*
The 2-year project was divided into two phases with each phase taking a different inquiry approach. In the first year (Phase 1), we built a Collaborative Inquiry Community (CIC) made up of nine teachers and two principals from Aotearoa New Zealand primary schools and five teacher educators with long-standing relationships with those school communities. Together we explored and built on the knowledge and

expertise of all members of the inquiry community regarding teaching for equity. In the second year (Phase 2) we focused on how we could use the knowledge generated in Phase 1 to inquire into, and improve, our practice with the learners we teach.

We started Phase 1 by exploring the concept of equity in teaching and learning contexts and examining the Facets of Practice for Equity (Facets) introduced in Chapter 1. We tested the Facets by describing and exploring examples of practice from our own experience of schooling as students, teachers, and teacher educators. We explored how the Facets were put into practice, including particular consideration of provision for children with special needs, normalising diversity, and challenging marginalisation. Notions of ako[4] (Bishop & Berryman, 2009) became important, as did the collection and analysis of evidence by teachers.

During the first year, teachers, principals, and three of the teacher educators met five times at each of the two schools. At key points we met as a full team and shared the knowledge built at each school site. As well as engaging in face-to-face discussion around equity, we trialled using an online knowledge-sharing platform in each school so that there could also be an asynchronous conversation. We set up Knowledge Forum software, which provides participants with opportunities to build knowledge by contributing ideas, practical theories, questions, examples, and counter-examples (Scardamalia & Bereiter, 2003). We were able to respond to each other's contributions, raising queries and adding information using a mind-map format and through attaching files. The software enabled us to trace the development of ideas across time and across the CIC. Later in Phase 1, in-school Google Docs were also used.

Although some members of the team identified that having different ways to join in allowed more voices to be captured and thus more equitable access to knowledge for people who work in different ways, the CIC team found the face-to-face discussions more productive than the online space. We found it easier to build knowledge face-to-face, using

---

4   Ako, the mutuality of teaching and learning, also acknowledges the importance of valuing the "knowledges and experiences" that both teachers and learners carry into the learning space (Berryman, Pennicott, & Tiata, 2018, p. 16).

the online environment as a place to keep a record of what had happened and to share examples of work. Our experience is summarised well in these quotes from two CIC teacher members:

> Teaching is inherently social so the social element is critical. It's the participation in the conversation that makes a difference—to relationships and learning.

> The face-to-face bit is implied in the Facets, so why wouldn't we expect this work to need face-to-face conversation?

One of the reasons for trialling an online platform for knowledge-building was to see if work of this sort could be done across schools where meeting face-to-face was difficult. Our experience suggests that working across schools is very productive and worthwhile, but that the need for trust and good relationships in order to confidently share practice and challenge each other requires face-to-face engagement.

These meetings and discussions resulted in the emergence of new shared knowledge about teaching for equity that was co-constructed by the group. A big idea that recurred in our discussions was the difference between equity and equality. Our work in Year 1 had heightened our personal and professional awareness of this difference and how equitable/inequitable practices influence the learning of diverse Aotearoa New Zealand students. As one of the deputy principals said:

> I think equity is a bigger picture thing than equality. Like, in terms of what the children have access to in our school, who does and who doesn't [have access] and how do we as teachers address that and go about making changes?

In the second year we took the Facets into school-based inquiries, exploring how they could be used to deepen practitioner inquiry and explicitly address inequity. At the end of Year 1 we set up three Collaborative Inquiry Teams (CITs). These CITs carried out inquiry projects to investigate how the knowledge built during the first year might be used to transform practice. Two were in-school CITs and one contained members from both schools. Each CIT included a university member. In the second year (Phase 2) the CITs met separately and worked on their inquiries. The CITs carried out cycles of data-gathering, analysis, and action using the Facets as a framework to guide what they looked at and how they carried out their inquiries.

The three inquiries used the Facets to explore how to:

1. improve teaching of mathematics and outcomes for learners
2. enhance communication with family and whānau[5] to better connect with students
3. address a spike in students' challenging behaviour.

The structure of the CITs was designed to enhance the agency of the participants, to address potential power issues, and to enhance access to resources and professional knowledge. Within the CITs, critical-friend relationships (Gibbs & Angelides, 2008) were established. Although each CIT determined the nature of their particular inquiry, all included observation, access to research information, and discussions and interpretations of data. The CIC continued to meet throughout this phase to share progress and ideas, and to consider data-collection techniques, analysis, synthesis, and critique.

At the start of Phase 2 we also explored what kinds of questions and data sources are useful for practitioner inquiry. We critiqued different kinds of questions and how the phrasing of research/inquiry questions determines the type of inquiry to be carried out. We considered how to narrow a broad focus into a narrower specific question, and how questions such as "What's going on here?" or "What's happening here?" lead to inquiries around "What happens if I ... ?"

We considered different ways of sourcing/gathering data to help us answer these questions, such as:

- interviews (with students, teachers, parents, community members, advocates)
- observations/shadowing (notes, recordings, journals)
- artefacts (student work, lesson plans / materials, communications, classroom documents)
- archival data (school data, records).

We also thought about the kinds of analysis appropriate for these different data sets, how to seek out the work of others for support and understanding, and the ethics of conducting practitioner inquiry.

---

5   Whānau—extended family/family group.

## *What we learnt about building an effective, strong inquiry community*

As we reflect on our work over 2 years, we realise that we have learnt the importance of creating a strong foundation on which to work. This includes building respectful and trusting relationships that enable open communication and sharing of ideas; recognition of the value of diversity in collaborative discussion; and careful development of shared understandings, in this case of the Facets of Practice for Equity. As we built our CIC, we acknowledged the significance of outsider and insider expertise and the importance of sufficient resourcing for the project to proceed. In this project, with its strong focus on inquiry, we identified different forms of practice-based inquiry and the importance of evidence to this work. These aspects of our project will be discussed in the following sections.

### Building a strong foundation

Looking back on the entire project, we found that our work in Phase 1 had built strong foundations on which to build the collaborative inquiries conducted in Phase 2. The foundations began with the establishment of working relationships across the groups. Through these working relationships, communicating and sharing ideas became a fruitful process of communal knowledge-building about how the Facets could guide equitable practice and how we might modify the wording of the Facets to make them clearer principles for practice. A helpful feature for extending our thinking and building knowledge together was the diversity of our team members.

### Building relationships

The significance of trust between team members in doing work of this sort cannot be underestimated. Trust may need to be developed in order to work across the "layers" of a school (for example, is it okay to show uncertainty in front of the principal?) or between schools where people need to get to know each other. Without trust there can be no productive conversation, especially about difficult or sensitive topics. Moving from friendly and relatively general conversations to an exchange of ideas specifically aimed at improving student learning entails risk-taking and trust as well as values of respect and reciprocity (Poskitt, 2005).

In this project, trust grew out of the time spent together exploring the topic of teaching for equity. We shared our sometimes painful experiences and became vulnerable. As Robinson, Hohepa, and Lloyd (2009) indicate, "Relational trust involves a willingness to be vulnerable because one has confidence that others will play their part" (p. 183). Over time, as the participants in the project learnt more about each other and gained confidence that the sharing of personal and professional experiences would stay within the CIC, the members became increasingly willing to share and discuss their professional challenges relating to equity. Less hierarchical relationships formed between them and they became "co-learning partners" (Lave & Wenger, 1991, p. 88). These working relationships involving trust were developed through regular meetings and knowledge-sharing, and can be described as whanaungatanga[6] (Education Council New Zealand | Matatū Aotearoa (2011)), which includes the concept of manaakitanga[7] as participants respected and cared for each other.

## Enabling open communication and sharing of ideas

Much is made of the idea that groups of people can share their ideas and build knowledge when they collaborate (Popp & Goldman, 2016). We also know that groups can talk "at" each other. In these circumstances, although sharing is occurring, the group does not develop new understandings through the talking process. For this reason, we looked carefully at two things: the processes that occurred in the group discussions that led to the building of new knowledge, and the evidence of knowledge-building in the online space we created.

We identified eight conversational moves that were linked with knowledge-building in the CIC. These were:

1. sharing examples
2. clarifying (rephrasing or inviting comment)
3. adding (providing additional information or examples)

---

6  Whanaungatanga—developing high expectations and respectful working relationships with students and the wider community.

7  Manaakitanga—demonstrating integrity, sincerity, respect, and care for others.

4. querying (seeking further information from others)
5. reflecting
6. theorising practice
7. considering implications (for learners, classes, teachers, schools, and whānau)
8. summarising (and/or affirming).

The online collaboration was different. The online space was used for summarising, synthesising, refining, building a repository for our work that we could return to, and saving and sharing artefacts (notes, photographs).

**Valuing diversity in collaborative discussion**

Diversity within our CIC was significant for building rich understandings of equity and equitable practice. Talking with only like-minded people rarely leads to challenge and new ideas. Diverse teams create more puzzles for their members and increase the effort needed to understand. In the act of trying to understand each other deeply, there is potential for growth. Diversity in this context might be cultural, but it might also include diversity of team members' roles in a school, or diversity of schools or institutions represented. Our group was culturally diverse, but it also included leaders *and* teachers from schools, and teacher educators (not only as researchers but as group members). This diversity ensured that a range of perspectives was present in the group and led to productive questioning and discussion. Each person had knowledge and expertise that could be contributed to the group. Therefore, a key task was making sure that all voices were heard and that everyone had space and time to contribute. This task was initially made possible by the university team leader and the school leaders who, by modelling inclusivity, enabled the team members to share knowledge and experiences. This process can be likened to the description by Berryman et al. (2018) of mauri[8] where it is recognised that everyone has knowledge to share and is open to increasing their own learning and that of others. Knowledge of pedagogical practice, curriculum, or subject matter (the "what" of the discussion) was matched with

---

8 Mauri—innate worthiness.

knowledge of ways to work that were culturally appropriate or of how to collect and analyse data (the "how" of the discussion). Knowledge was built in both of these domains (the "what" and the "how") during the collaboration.

We were also mindful that too much diversity can lead to talking past each other. It is important when putting together a group for this type of work to consider how you can balance enough overlap for communication to be functional and productive with enough diversity to stimulate genuine exchange of ideas. Thinking about voices that are sometimes missing from discussion can be a way to include new, stimulating perspectives in inquiry groups.

## Expanding our knowledge of the Facets

As described in Chapter 1, this study built on the Facets of Practice for Equity that had been developed in a previous study. They proved to be a helpful framework for opening discussion about practice for equity and for inquiring into practice. Without the framework to guide our thinking, we would have had discussions that were less focused and more difficult to learn from. We were able to tie new ideas back to the framework, and make links across key ideas using the Facets. Having an idea about why particular ideas or actions might be powerful and developing a shared vocabulary for discussing ideas are two benefits of having a conceptual framework. Another is being able to answer the perennial "So what?" question at the conclusion of inquiry phases. Findings can be discussed in terms of the conceptual frame, and what they add to knowledge can be identified using the framework's key ideas as an organising mechanism.

In addition, the Facets stimulated us to think of things we hadn't considered before, reminding us of aspects of practice that we might not have paid attention to without the framework. Often, we are "tuned in" to parts of practice that interest us or that we are concerned about. The Facet framework helped us to keep an open mind and think outside our own perspective.

The inherent integration of the Facets enabled us to consider and discuss the complexity and challenges of teaching for equity. For example, a new entrant teacher explained how the children bringing their home experiences to their school learning had influenced her lesson design. In her reading lesson sequences, she provided learning opportunities aligned to valued learning outcomes (Facet 1). However, other Facets impacted here as the teacher had deliberately developed an open classroom culture by inviting parents and whānau to participate in the classroom (Facet 3), and she also welcomed discussions that connected to the students' experiences (Facet 2). As she explained:

> The new entrants I find really interesting, so much [about the students] comes up during reading. During guided reading they are picking things out from pictures in the books. They always bring up their own interests and their own experiences that they can relate to and that gives you a huge amount of insight into what those kids do or are interested in, or are about to do. The classroom culture, the kind of culture you have got in your classroom, can enable or disable that kind of interaction. We are lucky with junior classes. We get a lot of parents coming in and bringing in the siblings.

It was during our discussions in Phase 1 that we realised that the wording of two of the Facets (2 and 6) needed to be changed or elaborated to capture the richness of teaching for equity. We discussed how it is not sufficient to simply connect to the children's lives and experiences; teachers also need to understand the learning of the children in their classroom. As a result of these discussions throughout Phase 1 we acknowledged that Facet 2 did not capture the full extent of the connections necessary. Facet 2, *Connecting to students' lives and experiences,* was therefore expanded to become **Connecting to students as learners, and to their lives and experiences.**

We also felt that Facet 6 needed to be reworded more strongly to indicate practitioners' crucial role in addressing inequitable practice in Aotearoa New Zealand's educational systems. Rather than simply challenging inequities, understood as "speaking out", our CIC believed the wording of Facet 6 should be a call to action. Thus Facet 6, *Recognising and challenging classroom, school, and societal practices that reproduce inequities*, was changed to ***Recognising and* seeking to address *classroom, school, and societal practices that reproduce inequity*.** "Seeking to address" indicates more directly than "challenging" that some action needs to occur. In our discussions we noted that seeking to address can involve changing personal behaviour; modelling behaviours for other children to follow when working alongside, for example, a child with special needs; and questioning inadequate systemic definitions, expectations, or provisions, at both school and national levels.

## Creating collaborative communities

The collaboration in this TLRI project was among two schools and a team of university-based teacher educators. The aim of the collaboration was to explore teaching for equity together, in a way that did not position anyone as holding superior knowledge. The teacher educators brought their reading and thinking from the literature, their research expertise, and their experience of practice with children and student teachers. The school-based team members brought their knowledge from reading and thinking and their experience of working with learners in diverse communities in low-socioeconomic areas of Auckland. The school-based teams comprised school principals, middle leadership, and classroom teachers, so the collaboration was also among the layers within each school, as well as across the two schools and with the teacher educators.

### Respecting outsider and insider expertise

As noted above, our CIC comprised teachers and leaders from two primary schools and five teacher educators from a university. Everyone brought knowledge and expertise to the collaboration, and the collaboration was designed to draw on all the different types of knowledge and expertise present in the group. School-based participants later identified the importance of the research expertise of the university participants in helping to make the inquiries more systematic and data informed. Knowledge of how to conduct research in school settings was useful for identifying sources of evidence and new ways of collecting information about students' experiences (Cordingley, 2015). Sometimes university staff are characterised as knowing about the outcomes of research (what the research says), but this collaboration highlighted the usefulness of also knowing *how* to research. The university staff were external to the schools' day-to-day functioning; however, they were embedded in the school teams for the collaboration. This made them trusted outsiders, which was a productive relationship. Having external people embedded in the school teams meant that taken-for-granted ways of working needed to be explained and thought about in more depth, and there was someone to report to about progress. We also had the opportunity to share expertise between the two schools. This sharing was valued by all the team members, as it also provided "trusted questioners" who could ask for clarification and add their own knowledge and experience to the discussion. In addition to the professional and research expertise of the CIC, we drew on Professor Marilyn Cochran-Smith's expertise in practitioner research and inquiry (Cochran-Smith & Lytle, 2009) when she was in Aotearoa New Zealand. We found that outside expertise provided new perspectives and prompted fresh thinking about ongoing challenges and patterns of behaviour related to teaching for equity.

**Resourcing**

Working in collaborative groups on big ideas is time consuming and difficult. Time was needed to build trust and share ideas in both the CIC and CITs. We needed to continually work together throughout the 2 years of the project to keep building shared understandings, question assumptions and findings, and maintain momentum. In our two very busy schools, finding space in the timetable was challenging. Resources needed to be provided if our work was to be effective. Funding from the TLRI project and time provided by the schools were both used to resource our collaborative work by releasing teachers from their classroom teaching to attend CIC meetings, to work together on their inquiries, and to meet to plan, discuss, and analyse their findings.

## *Learning about different forms of inquiry*

Insightful inquiry can take different forms. In education it is common for researchers to coin new terms and to promote particular ways of working. In this TLRI project we tried to gather together a range of perspectives on teacher inquiry and practitioner research in order to understand how they overlapped and what the key messages were. We looked at action research, critical action research, participatory action research, teacher research, self-study, and scholarship of teaching and learning. All these approaches centre on practice as the context for inquiry and position practitioners as generators of knowledge, notions which underpinned our project. In addition, in these approaches, issues arising from practice are the source of questions, and systematic data collection and analysis forms part of the research process. These approaches frame inquiry as a "project" to be done. In our work, we looked beyond this to "inquiry as stance" (Cochran-Smith & Lytle, 2009).

As outlined in Chapter 1, inquiry as stance describes an orientation towards practice where inquiry is seen as a critical habit of mind that teachers bring to all their work, rather than a one-off event or a set of steps. One of the reasons for undertaking structured inquiry is that it can foster inquiry as stance. Inquiry as stance motivates ongoing questioning of practice and understanding of how practice impacts students. According to Hynds and McDonald (2010), motivation is a key factor in causing teachers to change their teaching pedagogies. Everyone in this project brought a strong sense of inquiry as stance and, through the CIC discussions about the Facets, was further motivated to change their practice in order to improve student learning. Additionally, inquiry as stance, with its democratic purposes and social justice ends, aligned with our project's focus on teaching for equity.

Both these ideas about inquiry—inquiry as a stance or orientation, and inquiry as a systematic look into specific aspects of practice—were explored through the work of the CIC and CITs. Our first inquiry, undertaken together in the first year of the TLRI project, involved CIC members sharing their experiences of teaching for equity and using this data to interrogate the Facets. This was a whole-team inquiry, with the members sharing experiences and ideas from their different perspectives. The three school-based inquiries carried out in the second year of the project also encapsulated both ideas about inquiry. Each inquiry was motivated by a desire to improve equitable outcomes for students—inquiry as stance. Each inquiry also had a focusing question and systematic data-gathering and analysis processes about specific practices that moved the inquiry forward. The inquiries were shaped by the context in which they occurred and by the CIT that pursued them, which meant that the inquiries did not look the same.

We acknowledge that whatever the form of inquiry, practice is the context and that the practitioners within this context are constructed as researchers and knowledge generators. In this we were following a practitioner-teacher inquiry approach defined by Babione (2014) as "grounded in the realities of educational practice as teachers investigate their own questions and facilitate classroom change based on the knowledge discovered" (p. x).

## *Exploring and utilising evidence*

While evidence is an important aspect of inquiry, the use of data appears to be often neglected (Sinnema, Alansari, & Turner, 2018). In this project, we used evidence in different ways during the two phases. In the first phase, experiential evidence was used to test the validity and usefulness of the Facets. In the second, evidence was gathered to answer inquiry questions set by the CITs.

Data is not necessarily, or only, numbers and test results. In the three school-based inquiries, data came from observations, self-reflections, student voice, student work samples, interviews, and recording the frequency with which events occurred. Data were drawn from across the schools' communities—from students, teachers and senior school leaders, and parents and whānau. In order to avoid a common criticism of inquiry—that is, not collecting sufficient data on which to base conclusions and actions—the CITs were systematic in collecting and analysing data relevant to their inquiry questions. Collecting and analysing data added two considerations to the inquiry process that were very helpful for thinking and making changes to practice. We looked to see evidence of change in relation to the questions we asked. In our CITs, we asked lots of questions about the data we gathered and what this meant in terms of our inquiry foci. Analysing and discussing the data together as a CIT helped us answer the question "Have we made a difference?" Exchanging ideas about data and findings also helped us consider where we would go next in our inquiries. For us, data analysis was critical as it brought us back to our inquiry questions and opened up a space for being surprised about what we were finding. It also helped us question our assumptions about our school and classroom practices.

## *Summary*

In this chapter we have outlined what we learnt about developing a strong collaborative community for inquiry into teaching for equity. Our experience aligned with the literature on teacher inquiry

(Cochran-Smith & Lytle, 2009) and professional learning communities (Cordingley, 2015; Robinson et al., 2009). The Facets provided a stimulus to our thinking and a guide for what would be worthwhile to pursue in our inquiries. At the end of the first year of the project we formed three CITs to work on key questions that we would inquire into the following year (Phase 2). The following three chapters present each of the three inquiries as case studies, explaining what happened and further illustrating the features described in this chapter.

## Chapter 3
# Using the Facets of Practice for Equity to improve the teaching of mathematics

In this chapter, we describe how the within-school Collaborative Inquiry Team (CIT) at Fairburn School used the Facets of Practice for Equity (the Facets) in inquiries investigating aspects of teaching mathematics. We begin by situating the work we did in a wider context, to explain why it was important, and then we describe how we arrived at our inquiry questions, the steps we took in the inquiry, and the outcomes of our work for teaching practice and student learning.

Schools often select an area that the whole school will work on together for a year. Sometimes it's a curriculum area, such as writing or PE, and sometimes it's a broader issue, such as positive behaviour management or engaging parents with the school. At our school, the school-wide focus for the year was mathematics. We were asked to develop a new scheme of work for mathematics, moving away from our previous numeracy-based approaches towards using the full mathematics curriculum. Some of the teams in the school were working on what progress would look like at each year level.

Our CIT consisted of three teachers and one teacher educator. The three teachers in the CIT wanted to make sure that our inquiry fitted in with the work they needed to do on mathematics, and so mathematics teaching and learning became our curriculum context. Typically, an inquiry into mathematics teaching and learning might pursue questions such as "How can we improve student understanding of place value?" or "What is the impact of using computer-based mathematics tools on students' arithmetic knowledge?" We decided that our inquiry would focus on an area of mathematics that we had identified as problematic from assessment evidence. We would change our practice and then evaluate the impact of this changed practice. Some of the inquiries we were considering were linked to different ways of teaching place value and implementing an online learning programme. The Facets of Practice for Equity added a new dimension to these concerns. They suggested where changes might be made (by pointing out practices that are associated with improving equity for learners), and they added consideration of how current practice and proposed new practices might affect not only student outcomes, but also equity in relation to student outcomes. So, as a CIT, we considered how the school-wide focus on mathematics and the Facets could be brought together in an inquiry (see Figure 3.1).

Figure 3.1: **The relationship between the elements of *what* (curriculum focus), *why* (Facets of Practice for Equity) and *how* (through inquiry) in developing the Collaborative Inquiry Team's focus**

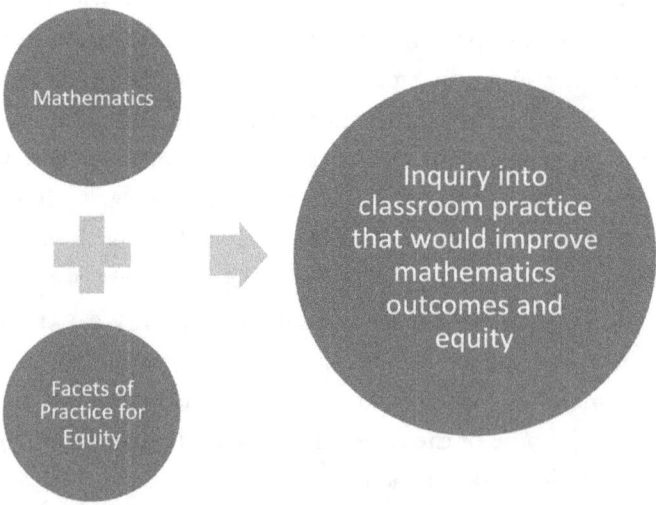

## *Using the Facets of Practice for Equity to think differently*

Considering the Facets shifted our conversation from "What mathematics can the students do/not do?" to "How does what we, as teachers, do in mathematics teaching impact how the students participate in mathematics learning, and their equity of access to important ideas in mathematics?" This extra dimension of the impact of practice on equity took our discussion in new directions.

Using the multifocal lens of mathematics and equity, a central issue emerged: differential participation in mathematics discussion. Our school is linguistically and culturally diverse, and there are many students for whom English is not their home language. In addition, acquiring or using the vocabulary needed to express mathematical ideas appeared to be challenging for junior and middle school students. Many of the new entrant students did not talk about ideas in class. Whether this was by choice or because they could not was not clear. Our observations of children in class showed us that this issue was still apparent at Year 3, where some very verbal students dominated discussions, while others remained silent. It was difficult to know how this impacted the learning of the quiet students.

We went to the literature and discovered that discussion and talk in mathematics classrooms has been identified as one of the key ways by which students come to understand both the content of mathematics and the ways in which mathematics is done (Anthony & Walshaw, 2007). Anthony and Walshaw (2009) listed 10 key evidence-based elements of effective mathematics teaching. Two of these are *mathematical communication* and *mathematical language*: facilitating ways of arguing and explaining that develop mathematical thinking, and facilitating the use of correct mathematical terms. We noted also that during mathematics professional development initiatives teachers are encouraged to employ "talk moves" (Chapin, O'Connor, & Anderson, 2014) to get students contributing their ideas and building on each other's thoughts, because this is seen as critical to the students' learning. Students' contributions are often used as formative assessment evidence, and "Tell me how you worked that out" is a frequent diagnostic technique. When students are not contributing orally in mathematics, it may impact their teacher's knowledge of their skills, their opportunities to learn from classroom discourse, and the development of their mathematics vocabulary.

We next considered what our understanding of the Facets added to this, by asking, "Who is talking and who is not talking?" We believed that if the "talkers" are going to learn more, then it is possible that the way we encourage talking might perpetuate inequity by marginalising some groups of students. This is a big question, and the more emphasis that is placed on talking as a way to learn mathematics, the more crucial it becomes. To find a way to tackle this big idea about inequity in the classroom, we turned again to the Facets of Practice for Equity. The six Facets provided a "short list" of places to look for changes in practice that might increase equity in access to ideas through oral participation in mathematics.

Two key areas arose from our discussion: the role of students' talk in *Using evidence to scaffold learning and improve teaching* (Facet 4) and *Connecting to students as learners, and to their lives and experiences* (Facet 2). *Using evidence to scaffold learning and improve teaching* linked to the importance of students' oral contributions in formative assessment processes. Without oral contributions, teachers have little evidence on which to build their teaching moment-to-moment. We all know how hard it is to tailor a question or task for a child who is not responding. We were also aware that in group situations where one or two students are confident speakers, it can be difficult to draw ideas out from other group members, or to prevent the group "going along" with the more orally confident students.

*Connecting to students as learners, and to their lives and experiences* linked to the teachers' awareness of students' home languages, which were languages that the CIT teachers did not speak. We wondered how much of the new entrant students' apparent reticence was because English was the language of the classroom, and how much was because they did not understand the ideas, did not know how to make a contribution, or did not feel safe to contribute. We also discussed the fine line between "requiring" extrovert behaviour, because talking is a key way to learn, and honouring students' personalities and approaches, which may be more introverted. However, if students are sitting back because barriers are preventing their participation, then we felt that this could create or perpetuate inequity. Overall, we believed that understanding more about the communication patterns in the classroom was a potentially important element of considering equity in the teaching of mathematics.

This led to the development of our two inquiry questions, one for the Year 3 class and one for the new entrants (which also involved Year 5/6 students as buddies).

- What happens if we buddy Year 1 and Year 5/6 students to do problem-solving? How does this enable us to connect to them as learners, and to their lives and experiences?
- What happens if I share evidence about students' problem-solving with the students? How does this enable me to scaffold learning and improve teaching?

Each question was double-barrelled. First, it included the exploration of a new practice designed to improve mathematics learning and equity of outcomes in mathematics. Secondly, it linked the new practice to a Facet of Practice for Equity, in order to bring the findings and discussion back to understanding how teaching practices can promote equity or perpetuate inequity. Next, we describe how each inquiry proceeded: what we did and what we found out.

## *Using buddies to build communication in mathematics*

This inquiry took up the key idea of learners' home languages, and the idea that child–child communication might have different patterns to adult–child communication. The tuakana–teina relationship[9] in te ao Māori (the Māori world), where older siblings or cousins help younger learners, provided a basic model for buddying older and younger students. This model also pairs more knowledgeable learners with novice learners. The older students were mostly proficient speakers of both English and their home languages, and therefore had more options for communicating with the Year 1 students. They also had relationships with many of the younger students, being siblings, cousins, or friends

---

9   A relationship in which an older or more expert tuakana (older sibling or cousin) guides a younger or less expert teina (younger sibling or cousin).

of family members. Our inquiry aimed to leverage the older students' linguistic skills and connections with the lives and experiences of the Year 1 students to increase opportunities for the younger students to talk about mathematics and use mathematical language.

Our first steps were very practical—we had to work out how to get the two classes to work together and how to collect information about what happened when they did. The question focused on problem-solving, an area of the curriculum that was being promoted by the school-wide professional learning activities. Given that problem-solving work often relies on group discussion and collaborative processes, it fitted our inquiry focus well. However, getting the Year 1 students started on problem-solving and having them talk about what they were doing proved challenging. The first session, therefore, focused on a problem-solving task, where the students had to work together to build towers to particular specifications. The Year 1 students and the Year 5/6 class were buddied up according to home language and any existing relationships that we were aware of. We planned to video what happened using iPads, so that we could look at the interactions in more detail after the session. We also planned to photograph the products of problem-solving (the towers) to see how successful the groups had been.

The first session made us realise that logistics were one of our challenges. There was a lot of noise and activity, and the space we had available was not large enough for both classes to work together on a hands-on activity of this sort. The logistics of gathering data about the impact of putting the students together was difficult, too: the noise made video difficult, and the photographs were static and did not capture language use. Two key things emerged, however: the younger students talked a lot more when working with the older buddies, and the students all chose to use English. Videoing students explaining what they had done was a useful way of capturing some of the increased participation of the younger students, as with the support of their older buddies they were excited to explain the towers they had made. The younger students had a responsive, enthusiastic older child encouraging them to speak and many students who did not contribute in larger class discussions were observed talking in sentences in the smaller groups.

Taking what we had learnt from this first cycle of inquiry, we shifted our focus to measurement in mathematics, an area where vocabulary becomes particularly significant. We thought that links could be made by buddies between home language words that students might know and English terms. We also thought that a chance to use the key words repeatedly in a small group situation would enhance the Year 1 students' learning. The students worked in pairs or groups of three to compare objects in the classroom and make statements about "longer" and "shorter"; for example, "The pen is shorter than the desk." For this activity, the younger students visited the older students' classroom. This time we gave the iPads to some of the older students to record what they could see happening. The inquiry team members also worked around the classroom, observing the language used and asking questions of the older and younger students when appropriate.

In this second cycle, we observed that the students again used English, but that the younger students were more voluble and participated verbally with unexpected competence in the paired / small group situation. They had many more opportunities to use the terms "longer" and "shorter" than they would have had in a whole class activity with only one or two adults to guide them. After this cycle, we discussed the tuakana role that the 25 older children took, noting that some were very comfortable in this role while others were less so. This led us to think more about the opportunities offered to the older children by the buddying-up exercise, and we agreed that we needed to talk to the tuakana about how they could take on the role in more sophisticated ways.

In the third iteration, we kept the idea of measurement comparison and moved the activity outside. Using outside spaces proved to be helpful in reducing distraction and confusion from high noise levels and gave the buddy groups more room to talk and explore. The task was to compare the Year 1 students' heights to objects around the school, using "taller" and "shorter" (e.g., "Rewi is shorter than the ladder"). To increase accountability for the older students we gave each group an iPad on which they had to record their Year 1 student making comparison statements. This proved highly motivating for both the tuakana and the teina students, and provided us with excellent data. We were able to watch the videos and notice when students who were not contributing orally in the classroom situation were able to do so in this setting. All the teina students were able to make comparison statements on the videos and clearly had multiple opportunities to encounter and explore the idea with their tuakana buddy. In this iteration, we also tried asking the Year 1 students one-on-one, before and after the buddy session, some questions about what they had learnt and about comparison in measurement. The Year 1 students' apparent increased confidence in talking did not extend to this activity, however, and it was difficult to get useful data in this way. This was further evidence of the power of creating different communication structures in the classroom.

When a new Year 1 class began in Term 3, we felt that the tuakana–teina model might help in this setting as well, as the older students had increased their confidence in the tuakana role. A group of tuakana visited the new Year 1 classroom at mathematics time to help teach the 5-year-old students how to do independent mathematics activities. This was very successful, increasing the engagement of the younger students and the amount of on-task talk that occurred in independent work. It gave an opportunity for the teacher to observe what her new students were capable of orally when they were talking with a student buddy, rather than with the teacher or in front of the class.

We also wondered what the tuakana students thought about helping the younger ones with their mathematics learning, so we asked them to complete a small survey. The tuakana students reported increased confidence as a result of being in the teacher role, and a sense of pride and pleasure at being involved in the learning of others.

## Sharing evidence with learners

The second inquiry, undertaken in a Year 3 classroom, took up the problem-solving focus of the whole-school professional learning in a different way. In this class, the CIT-member teacher had similar concerns to those of the Year 1 teacher: there was low overall participation in mathematical discussions, with only very confident students contributing their ideas. The teacher was concerned about the mathematical vocabulary of the students and their ability to put their ideas into words. Did they know the concept, but were unable to express it? Or were they unable to access the concepts because of not having the vocabulary to discuss the ideas?

This inquiry focused on how evidence of problem-solving could be used with students to improve their participation in discussions and build their mathematics vocabulary. We selected this focus because teachers often use evidence from students' work to make their decisions about what to teach next and how to teach it. However, it is less common to share this process with the students, despite it giving them agency in their learning and the opportunity to learn from reflecting on evidence themselves.

To begin the inquiry, the students worked in small problem-solving groups to undertake a geometry task. The students had to make different shapes using pipe cleaners, and explain what the features of the shape were. The students struggled with making rectangles, being unsure of the definition, and in some cases were unable to work together to make the shape. In order to gain some evidence that we could consider and to provide stimulus for the next stage of the inquiry, we filmed the students as they worked, using iPads.

Figure 3.2: **Students working together to make shapes with pipe cleaners**

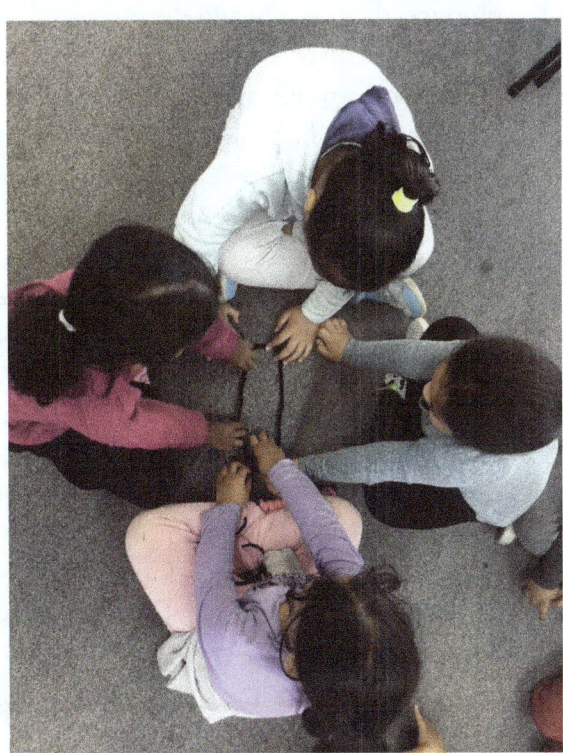

In the next stage of the inquiry, the class came together in their groups to watch the videos of themselves working. The first time through they watched without the sound on, allowing them to provide a commentary and discuss what they could see. The video could be stopped and started easily, permitting further talk about what the students could see in the evidence they were working with. The students engaged readily with this. In discussion they noticed aspects of the mathematics they were working on (for example, "That's not a rectangle"), and aspects of their group work (for example, "Rewi hasn't said what he thinks"). We then gave the students the opportunity to attempt the activity again, and they were much more successful.

The inquiry proceeded, using video, photographs, and artefacts of student work as objects for reflection for both students and teachers. In essence, this provided further opportunity for the students to learn from an activity they had engaged in. The students participated once as group members and then had the chance to look at what happened and to build their metacognition about their achievements/progress through reflecting on the products they created and the processes they used. We found that watching video without sound was a particularly productive way to generate and explore vocabulary, as it provided opportunities to introduce and reinforce specific terms, and for students to practise using these. Pictures with no sound invite talk, and they proved to be a stimulating way to get mathematical discussion happening.

We also used photographs in this inquiry as a way for students to return to and use new vocabulary to explain what was happening in the pictures. We found that providing the students with regular opportunities to return to photographs and examples of their work encouraged them to build their mathematical vocabulary and built their ability to explain their ideas. Our inquiry evidence sources became prompts for, and records of, extended mathematical discussion, which otherwise might have disappeared.

This inquiry proceeded through four cycles, using different provocations to begin the students' work (using balances to measure weight, exploring the distances between the stars in Matariki,[10] number talks, and pentominoes). In each case, a rich task was presented to

---

10  Matariki is commonly known as star cluster Pleiades. See, e.g., Matamua, (2017).

the students, evidence was collected from their work (video, photographs, or artefacts such as recording of strategies or drawings), and this evidence was shared with the students as a starting point for deeper discussion and a "second chance" to learn. Over the four cycles, new patterns of student participation emerged, with greater numbers of students contributing to discussion and an increase in the use of mathematical terms to describe ideas. The supported second-chance opportunity changed the pattern of talk because the students could refer to an artefact and talk from their experience, rather than being asked to contribute to a discussion which they might not be able to access. Everyone had been part of the learning experiences, so everyone had something they could say.

## What can be learnt from our experience of using the Facets of Practice for Equity and Inquiry to tackle inequity in mathematics teaching and learning?

All contexts are different, and the particular ideas that we picked up on will not necessarily be appropriate in other classrooms or schools. So what can be learnt from what we did? First, when we think about our classroom practice, we need to think about how we can improve student outcomes, but alongside that we need to ask whose outcomes will be improved and whether some students will be disadvantaged by the changes we might make. In the Year 3 class, the inquiry into using evidence of the students' problem-solving to co-construct "Where to next?" with the students raised questions and ideas that led to further cycles of inquiry. This became a continual process. The teacher's thinking behind this was, "Okay, when I used the problem-solving evidence it really worked for these children, but these other children were still not getting the idea. I think I'll try …". Continually inquiring into the impact of her actions on all the students in her class meant that new ideas, and ways to use evidence and scaffold learning, emerged throughout the year.

Secondly, using the Facets as a lens to focus our inquiries made the inquiries deeper, and we got into more powerful questions and ideas than if we had stayed at the level of improving an aspect of mathematics. Mathematics was important, though. In the CIT were teachers with different levels of confidence in mathematics (including one of the school's mathematics leaders), and the teacher educator was a mathematics education specialist. This diversity of expertise enriched the inquiry, and the team were able to bring together their collective knowledge and experience as they looked at the outcomes for students and decided what to do next. Having expertise in the context of the inquiry helped us make choices about what to do and to understand our impact in more depth. Others wanting to do this work would benefit from constructing teams that have expertise in the area of focus, and then layering a conceptual framework, such as the Facets, into the inquiry to deepen thinking and increase the significance of the outcomes.

Thirdly, inquiry of this sort takes time and energy, which can be in short supply in busy schools and classrooms. Having to be systematic about gathering and analysing data on our inquiry work was worthwhile but challenging. We have to acknowledge that, as is often the case, in writing about what we have done, some of the potholes and other roadblocks have been smoothed out. To engage in inquiry and thinking of this sort needs resourcing of time within the school: time to work out what to do differently, time to discuss deeply what is being discovered and learnt, and time to build a supportive inquiry group that can challenge and acknowledge along the way. Teacher learning will be more powerful when there is a chance to share it regularly and in low-key ways with colleagues who are on a similar journey.

## Chapter 4
# Enhancing equity through connecting to students as learners, and to their lives and experiences

In this chapter, we describe how one within-school Collaborative Inquiry Team (CIT) from New Lynn School conducted several cycles of inquiry to build more equitable outcomes for students. The focus was on building stronger partnerships with parents and whānau, an important dimension of Facet 2, *Connecting to students as learners, and to their lives and experiences*. The research question that prompted the inquiry was "How well do we communicate with family and whānau to connect with students as learners, and to their lives and experiences?" As an inquiry group, we had for some time been looking for ways to connect much more closely in partnership with students and their families in order to know and understand them in context. Even though our school makes great efforts to connect with parents and whānau, some families have had less than fruitful schooling experiences and we have, at times, found it challenging to build relationships.

We begin by explaining how we explored our existing relationships with parents and whānau to take stock of what we were already doing in relation to Facet 2. Next, we describe the questionnaire we designed and implemented to gather information from parents and whānau about their perspectives on partnership and involvement with their children's schooling. Based on the stocktake and the information from the questionnaire, we extended some existing connections practices and designed and implemented others. Each of these practices is described before we present findings from a second round of data gathering. We conclude the chapter with a discussion about what we discovered through conducting our inquiry, its limitations, and implications for our future practice.

## Taking stock of our partnership with students, families, and whānau

As part of the first year of the Teaching and Learning Research Initiative (TLRI) project that is the genesis of this book,[11] we had investigated the critical importance of building partnerships with families and whānau (see Chapter 2). This work led us to develop new ways of building these partnerships in order to make better links with all students within our two classrooms and syndicates. During the first year of the TLRI project, we spent time brainstorming ways in which we already tried to connect with our students' lives and families. We began by analysing these attempts and the issues we still faced, finding out what seemed to be difficult in making connections, and coming up with ways to address these issues. In particular, we identified that communication mostly seemed to be in one direction—from school to home. Figure 4.1 reproduces the list we brainstormed at this stage of the inquiry.

Figure 4.1: **List of school–home connections prior to beginning the inquiry**

| Notes from the school–home connections analysis | |
|---|---|
| • fortnightly school newsletters<br>• term syndicate newsletters<br>• homework sheets<br>• meet the teacher (early in Term 1)<br>• invitations to make an appointment sent with progress and anniversary reports<br>• e-portfolios on Seesaw | • permission slips for trips<br>• fundraising notes, emails, texts—about sports days, discos, camp meetings (Years 5 and 6 parents)<br>• reports<br>• merit certificates<br>• school and class web pages. |

---

11 "Teaching for Equity: How do we do it?" was a 2-year project funded by the Teaching and Learning Research Initiative. The final report for the project is available from the TLRI website http://www.tlri.org.nz/tlri-research/research-completed/cross-sector/teaching-equity-how-do-we-do-it

As the list demonstrates, teachers in our syndicate teams were making strong efforts to communicate with families. Unfortunately, requests for parents and whānau to contact the school were not often responded to, and the teachers thought that parents and whānau were not interacting through the electronic portfolios. Teachers believed they knew very little about their students' interests and experiences. This presented a problem if they were to attempt to design learning activities that connected with their students' lives and cultures.

In particular, we identified a problem with homework. As one teacher wrote in her field notes:

> There was very little homework being returned to school. The homework that was being done was often of poor quality, in books that had not been cared for. Teachers felt disheartened as they were spending time creating homework sheets, photocopying them off, handing them out, reminding, giving incentives, then getting few back.

To investigate the homework issue more deeply, we designed a survey for parents and whānau which asked what they believed would work best for them and their children (see Figure 4.2). The survey comprised five questions. We mostly wanted to hear parents' opinions and so the items were open ended, although parents could tick options if preferred. We sent the survey home to all families in the two syndicates and had a very pleasing return rate, enough to assist us in designing a new approach.

Gratifyingly, in the senior syndicate, nearly 100% of the surveys were returned, and there was an 80% return in the middle syndicate. The responses indicated that most parents wanted their children to have homework, and they wanted opportunities for "passion projects" where children could follow their own interests. Parents also asked for a longer period of time to work on these projects, rather than within a week. They also suggested different forms of presentation, such as slideshows, models, posters, and photo stories. To address these findings, we initiated a new way to approach homework and changes to how we used digital communication systems in our syndicates. The two major initiatives were an innovative homework system designed to bring the children's lives into the classroom and the re-ignition of the electronic portfolio as a two-way communication tool.

Figure 4.2: **Homework survey for parents and whānau**

## Parent Survey – Homework

Would you like your child to have homework or would you prefer to have family time and time to get outside? Please complete this survey so that teachers can create homework that best matches your child's needs.

1. We prefer choices that include reading, maths, and spelling.
   *Tick or write a comment in the box*

2. We prefer choices that include manaakitanga—helping others—together with reading, maths, and spelling.
   *Tick or write a comment in the box*

3. We prefer the opportunity to do a "passion project", which could be shared online, and could be a model, poster, or writing.
   *Tick or write a comment in the box*

4. We do not want homework. We prefer to have family time and time to get outside.
   *Tick or write a comment in the box*

5. This is what we would like for homework:
   *Write a comment in the box*

We will collate this information and go with the majority.

## *Investigating new approaches to homework*

In the senior syndicate, we introduced one compulsory homework activity each week and eight different optional activities that students and their parents and whānau could choose from and collaborate on together. In both middle and senior syndicates, we changed the period in which the homework was due so that there was time for working parents to engage with their children to complete the activities. Instead of requiring homework within the working week, we extended the period over the weekend, making it due the following Monday. This suggestion was made by the parents in their feedback in the survey.

In the middle syndicate, the new approach was to have a set assignment in a basic subject each week and invite the students to complete an optional project on a subject related to their lives and experiences, based on a letter of the alphabet. For example, when the letter was "B", a family who live in a relatively rural setting picked blackberries and made jam together, then brought the jam to school. Another family made special biscuits and shared them and the recipe with everyone for morning tea. Prior to this approach, we didn't know about these family interests and their expertise in jam-making and baking.

Other families worked with their children to make models that represented aspects of their lives and interests. For example, in conversations designed to investigate the success of the new homework approach, students talked about how they collaborated with family to create the homework projects. For example, one student brought along a model giraffe (see Figure 4.3). When asked how she and her family went about the project, she told us:

> My family are all enjoying working together as a whānau to complete a homework project. I am the "director" and I make the choice of topic. Aunty is the artistic one and Grandma is the one who checks the facts and makes sure everything is correct. We've all enjoyed learning together and it's great to bring in projects as a team! This giraffe was sewn by Aunty and the facts are typed on paper, rolled up inside the neck.

Figure 4.3: **Example of a homework project**

In both syndicates, our inquiry was designed to capture the effects of the new homework approaches. Teachers in both syndicates noted that there was a clear improvement in the quality of the homework produced, and that more students were participating through these new options. Pleasingly, there was increased parental and whānau participation in the project work and students were excited and motivated by the approach. Some very creative and interesting projects arrived at school and provided the focus for conversations about student interests and cultural experiences (see Figure 4.4 below for examples).

In relation to Facet 2, as teachers, we learnt a great deal about the lives and backgrounds of our students, and were then able to prepare more worthwhile and relevant activities to engage them. For example, one student brought a model illustrating the Samoan legend of Sina and the eel, prompted by the letter "S" for homework that week. The display contained the legend, some weaving of leaves related to the story, and coconut shells to represent the moral of the story, in which the eel tells Sina he will provide food and drink for her through the coconut wherever she goes (a reference to the ubiquity of coconut trees throughout the Pacific Islands). The student's teacher built on this

Chapter 4 Enhancing equity through connecting to students as learners, and to their lives and experiences

project by reading the legend about Sina and the eel to the class. This gave the student mana[12] in the room. He had shared something that many could connect with. This, in turn, motivated more students to contribute homework projects and helped him to connect more and contribute further homework to the class. Prior to bringing this project along, he had done very little homework and had found school challenging.

Figure 4.4: **Examples of student/parent collaborative projects from the senior syndicate**

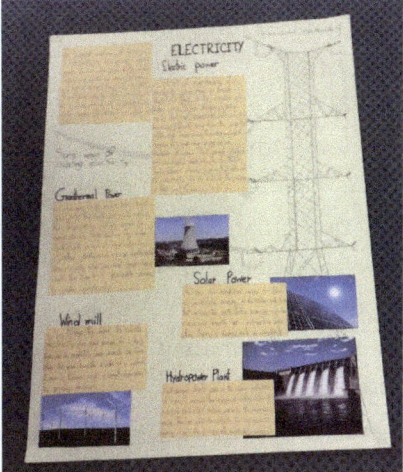

---

12  Mana—in te reo Māori—means power, effectiveness, and prestige.

In a similar vein, when asked "How does this new homework approach tell us more about you and your family?", students in one of our classes responded:

> Sometimes in the drawings—you know the cheetah one? I didn't draw that, my mum did. I chose India because my mum and dad come from there.

> My mum does the drawing and I do the writing. We work together.

As teachers, we wanted to celebrate this collaborative approach because it was great to see the parents and whānau involved in their children's learning and it gave us an insight into the students' lives and interests.

Following what we believed was a successful implementation of the new homework approach, we talked with the parents and whānau at our parent–teacher meetings about how it was working for them. We also gathered other evidence to help us assess how successful the new approach had been, such as tracking how much homework was produced each week and by whom, and monitoring interactions with parents and whānau to see if these had increased. Our findings are listed in Figure 4.5.

Figure 4.5: **Findings post-implementation of the new homework approaches**

| Outcomes after implementing the new homework approaches |
| --- |
| • All parents want homework. |
| • Some parents would like extra maths homework—we referred them to websites. |
| • Students do not feel so pressured, as teachers are flexible about accepting and sharing homework at any time. |
| • Interaction with parents has increased. |
| • Passion projects allow parents to share their talents. |
| • About 80% of students are completing homework each week. |
| • More parents are coming into the school and interacting with teachers. |
| • Teachers know more about and can connect more with our students. |

## Changes to the use of digital communication systems

Another strand of our inquiry was the introduction of increased digital communication with parents and whānau, including through texts, emails, and the e-portfolio system Seesaw. Our aim was to use these avenues to provide positive information for families about their children's progress and activities.

Prior to this intervention, our phone calls to parents often went unanswered. Our investigations suggested that parents and whānau often did not pick up phone calls from teachers. Maybe seeing the school number on their phone made them worry about possible bad news. Maybe parents needed more information to entice them to hear more. Whatever the reason, we began to send text messages that provided information first and then asked for a specific response. We also revitalised the use of Seesaw, our e-portfolio system. To do this, we sent out new codes that the parents needed to join the Seesaw system. We also offered an email service to help them with their questions about getting connected to Seesaw and training sessions at school with information about using Seesaw. We also encouraged parents and whānau to come to class at any time so that we could help them join up and use the system while at the school.

We involved the students more in adding contributions to Seesaw. For example, we encouraged students to upload short videos in which they explained maths ideas or showed their parents science experiments. We tried to ensure that new items were appearing in each student's portfolio throughout the term rather than the teachers uploading a set of four items per student once a term. This more organic approach, where both teachers and students uploaded items on a daily or weekly basis, appeared to encourage parents to respond more regularly and more fully. Parents had a starter to talk with their children about what they'd been doing at school and a way to discuss next steps.

## *Findings from our inquiries*

Data collected before we began and after two terms of implementation demonstrated a distinct change in the interaction patterns between home and school in our two classrooms and syndicates. As a result of the homework projects, we were able to plan lessons, choose appropriate resources, and interact more competently with our very diverse students, because we knew so much more about them, their lives, where they were from, and their cultures. The use of mobile and digital devices brought families into the school who had not visited before, and parents and children alike interacted virtually through Seesaw.

Through working as a team within the school, and together with our university partners, we have built much stronger relationships with students and their whānau and now know far more about their interests, skills, and relationships.

The Facets of Practice for Equity really made us think about the reasons why different learners might be marginalised. In the past we were aware of the more obvious reasons, such as health conditions or disabilities. However, working through the Facets as a team of classroom teachers and university researchers helped everyone concerned have a deeper understanding of the ways in which students and their families can be impacted. Working together as a CIT was an important success factor. It would have been harder if there weren't other staff members doing the inquiry. As one of the teachers explained, "The process definitely provided me with professional development. We worked together in syndicates to change our practices and, in the CIT, we explored both the inquiry process and the innovations we were implementing".

Another benefit of working as an inquiry team was the opportunities provided by the larger project for sharing outside the school context, for example in project meetings at the university. As one teacher put it:

> I liked being able to be off-site [at project meetings] so distractions were reduced and I could be more focused on the inquiry discussions. Going into the university made me take off my teacher's hat, so to speak, and helped me raise myself to a more academic level.

We began to talk about how the inquiry process might inform our work in a more formal community of learning. For example, we talked about the idea that a community of learning should have some kind of meeting space that would have the same effect as our trips to the university. Perhaps, for everyone to experience the advantages of off-site meetings, collaborative inquiry meeting locations could be rotated between schools.

An enduring outcome of the CIT project has been our commitment to equity. A recent example of this concerned a unit on fair play taught within one classroom. One teacher uses an equity v. equality picture discussed in the CIC as a touchstone to remind herself of the difference between equality and equity, and how the Facets can be vehicles to help provide not just an equal playing field, but one that assists students in ways they need to achieve and thrive. She explained how the experience of learning about the Facets and conducting the inquiry within these two syndicates has become an important aspect of her everyday thinking:

> I carry an equity picture in my head. It helps me remember the difference between equity and equality. And I use this in my teaching. I actually have a picture that I use with other teachers, students, and families to explain what I mean. [See Figure 4.6]

Figure 4.6: **Equality and equity**

(Source: Interaction Institute for Social Change: Artist Angus Maguire, developed from an image by Craig Froehle)

## Conclusions

Our approach to inquiry through this project changed aspects of how we went about our work. Our focus was on ways of knowing more about the learning, lives, and cultures of our students. The changes to the homework systems and to digital communications including e-portfolios brought us into much closer contact with our students' lives. We learnt a great deal not only about their lives and interests, such as when new projects arrived in the classroom, but also about who lived with them and who their whānau were. We got to know some of their family members more deeply and thus could communicate more effectively with them, which helped improve the support and attention our students got with their work. Perhaps more importantly, we learnt how to use inquiry as a collaborative team in ways that informed new ways of teaching towards more equitable outcomes.

# Chapter 5
# Cross-school collaborative inquiry to address school-wide problems of practice

In this chapter, we show how a cross-school Collaborative Inquiry Team (CIT), comprising deputy principals from Fairburn and New Lynn School and a teacher educator, investigated school-wide problems of practice. Following our work in the first year of the Teaching and Learning Research Initiative (TLRI) project,[13] we decided to focus our inquiries on Facet 6: *Recognising and seeking to address classroom, school, and societal practices that reproduce inequity.* We chose this focus because we believed our leadership roles included a responsibility to bring about system change for the benefit of all the children in our schools. We decided to work together as a CIT because we had noticed a marked increase in children exhibiting challenging behaviour in our two schools. We were concerned about equity issues related to opportunities to learn for those children, as well as about the impact of the challenging behaviour on the learning of other students in our schools.

---

13 "Teaching for Equity: How do we do it?" was a 2-year project funded by the Teaching and Learning Research Initiative. The final report for the project is available from the TLRI website http://www.tlri.org.nz/tlri-research/research-completed/cross-sector/teaching-equity-how-do-we-do-it.

We begin this chapter by describing how we undertook our first inquiries to help us find out why there had been a spike in children with challenging behaviour. We then explain how our data analysis led to our second inquiries. Our second inquiries were not the same as each other because the data showed that the triggers for children's challenging behaviour were different for each school. Finally, we describe how we worked as a cross-school CIT and what we learnt through undertaking our inquiries to help us address inequitable classroom and school practices.

## Finding out what was going on in our schools

There are two broad types of practitioner research questions that determine the kind of inquiry to be undertaken. These are (1) "What's going on here?" and (2) "What happens if …?" The first type of question focused our initial inquiries because we wanted to find out what was going on with the increased number of students exhibiting challenging behaviour. We wanted to see if, in terms of the challenging behaviour, classroom and school practices were reproducing inequities. However, as shown below, our specific questions related to the system used in each of our schools to address incidents of children's challenging behaviour.

- Fairburn has a "white stick" system. Each teaching space has a white stick that is used when a teacher needs extra support because of disruptive student behaviour, as well as health or other emergencies. The stick is taken by a student selected by the teacher to the front office. A member of the Senior Management Team (SMT) then goes to the teacher who requires assistance. The sticks are clearly labelled to indicate which teaching space/teacher they have come from. The questions for the first inquiry in this school were "Why is there an increased number of white-stick callouts, and are there consequences for reproducing inequity?"

- At New Lynn School, a member of the SMT—normally the Deputy Principal (DP)—deals with children who are causing extreme behavioural difficulties in class. The questions for the first inquiry in this school were "Why are more children being sent to the SMT because of challenging behaviour, and how will reducing this address classroom and school practices that reproduce inequities?"

Working together as a CIT we decided what data we would need to collect to help us answer our school-specific questions, and the best way to collect those data. Through Google Docs, we then collaboratively developed data-tracking sheets related to our own contexts. We wanted to design tracking sheets that were easy to understand and use because we wanted to ensure we were getting reliable data about what was going on in each of our schools. Because of contextual differences, the processes and outcomes of the CIT inquiries are discussed separately below.

**Fairburn**

The "Behaviour and Support" tracking sheet we developed was used to record every white-stick incident over a 2-week period. One member of the CIT worked with closely with the SMT to ensure that they were on board, as she explains:

> Because this [inquiry] was looking at classroom and school practices, I had to ensure that the SMT understood what I was doing. I would need their support with gathering information if we wanted to address the practices causing the problems.

Our CIT then met to analyse and discuss the data gathered via the tracking sheet. As shown in Table 5.1, there were 36 white-stick incidents relating to five main areas of challenging behaviour. Some white-stick incidents had multiple causes. Non-compliance (25 incidents) and deliberately disturbing other children (15 incidents) were the most frequently recorded behaviours. The data also showed that the time taken by members of the SMT to address these incidents of challenging behaviours came to approximately 11 hours over the 2-week period. Our CIT also noted that that the 36 white-stick incidents came from the senior area of the school.

Table 5.1 **Summary of white-stick incidents over a 2-week period**

| Analysis of incidents (students presented with one or more) |
| --- |
| NC (non-compliance): 25 |
| L (left the room): 6 |
| A (angry/upset): 6 |
| V (violence towards others/property): 2 |
| D (deliberately disturbing others): 15 |
| Total number of white-stick incidents: 36 |

We also collected information from the teacher or the child about what happened before the white-stick incident. The data showed a variety of triggers for the challenging behaviour, including some students not understanding or not being able to do the task, or not having the skills to work independently. Other students had difficulty with regulating their emotions.

During our CIT data-analysis discussions, we wondered if teachers across the school had a shared understanding of the purpose of the white sticks. We decided to interview eight teachers about what they thought the white stick was for. The most common responses were that white sticks were used when the teacher needed support because of safety issues, such as when the teacher's behaviour-management strategies had been exhausted, and because of student defiance and disrespect.

We also wondered about students' understanding of the white-stick process so we interviewed five students who had been "white-sticked" during the 2 weeks of data gathering. They said that it was used "when you are bad" and for medical emergencies. The students also said they didn't like the white stick and that it made them angry when they got sent out of class because of it.

The next step we took was to share the data with the syndicate that had the greatest number of white-stick incidents. We asked them to comment on why they thought there were more white sticks from that particular area of the school. The teachers suggested a number of reasons, including lack of experience teaching that age group, teacher stress, learning expectations for the students being too difficult and/or not clearly expressed, lack of sufficient scaffolding for the children to reach the next level, and external factors such as school events.

We then discussed the direction for our next inquiry, which would address a "What happens if …?" practitioner research question. Taking account of the information from all the data sources, we thought that the spike in challenging behaviour could be in part because the students were struggling to work independently on the tasks they were given. This led to the focus of our second inquiry: "What happens to the level of white-stick callouts if we prepare students to become more independent learners?"

We prepared for this inquiry by reading and talking with teachers and among our CIT about ways to build independence in learners. We decided to use a "must-do/can-do" strategy[14] that involved deciding what activities students "must do" in a specified time frame and the activities they "could do" once the required activities were completed. We thought this would help increase students' agency by supporting them to take ownership over their learning. A colleague who had successfully used this approach stressed it was critical that learning activities were purposeful and at the level of the learners.

Given staffing changes in the senior syndicate, we decided to trial the strategy with a teacher who was interested in increasing independence in her Year 2 students. She volunteered to work on the inquiry over the term. We decided to implement the inquiry during mathematics because that was our school-wide professional learning focus for the year. Because we were trialling the strategy and wanting to make the inquiry manageable, we decided to work with one group in the class. During each inquiry session the teacher worked with the students to list both the must-do and can-do activities. Because we wanted to motivate the children to complete the required tasks, the can-do menu included favourite activities identified by the children in the trial group.

Analysis of the data over the term showed that no children in that class had been white-sticked, and interviews with the teacher indicated that the group demonstrated greater independence as learners and

---

14 Te Kete Ipurangi (n.d.) http://elearning.tki.org.nz/Teaching/Inclusive-classrooms/Universal-Design-for-Learning/Planning-for-differentiated-learning

more responsibility when undertaking tasks. She commented that the children were more engaged and focused, that this gave her more time to work with the other children, and that the rest of the class was more settled.

It should be acknowledged that the can-do/must-do strategy took time to set up and a lot of effort to sustain over the term of trialling. However, the positive outcomes in terms of increased learner independence and no students being white-sticked during the trial led to discussions about how we could use what we had learnt to develop programmes to build other students' skills in being independent learners.

Being part of the TLRI project and undertaking the inquiries also led to discussions about the effects of our teaching practices on our students. We have become more focused on reducing inequities through looking at how our classroom and school practices can support all students to consistently engage with and participate in classroom learning activities and opportunities.

**New Lynn School**

As noted earlier in this chapter, our cross-school CIT's initial inquiry questions arose from our shared problem of practice—a marked increase in students' challenging behaviour in both our schools. To help answer the research question "Why are more children being sent to SMT because of challenging behaviour?" we collected data over a 2-week period. In line with our CIT discussions, a record was made of each child with challenging behaviour who had been sent by a teacher to an SMT member. The data captured the name and class level of the child, date and time of incident, description of the incident/behaviour, what happened before the incident, and what the consequences were. Table 5.2 summarises what the data revealed.

Table 5.2 **Summary of incidents of challenging behaviour where children were sent to an SMT member over a 2-week period**

| Total number of incidents | 63—includes 13 children with more than one incident |
|---|---|
| Description of incidents | Non-compliance—26<br>Hurting other children—14<br>Swearing/teasing—10<br>Disrespect—5<br>Running off from class—8 |
| Class levels of incidents | Senior school—34<br>Middle school—24<br>Junior school—5 |
| Time when most incidents occurred | 11.40–1.10 p.m. (Writing time in the senior school) |

As the data in Table 5.2 shows, many of the behaviour incidents occurred during writing time. This was very important information for the SMT that we had not noticed before. Also, many of the incidents came from the senior school.

As we were interested in student perspectives, we asked a random sample of 15 students from the middle and senior school who had appeared in the data about their class and school experiences, including their likes and dislikes. Many of them expressed a strong dislike of writing. We then focused on the views of senior school students and surveyed 20 students about what they liked and didn't like about writing. These included students who had been sent to an SMT and those who had not. Individual student comments included:

- I like writing about animals because I learn new things.
- I like writing about what I want to write about.
- I like writing about different things but it is hard because I don't know what to write about.
- I like writing about animals but I hate to have to write a procedure like a recipe.
- I don't like writing because I can't write nicely and hate having to write about what the teacher says. I want to write about rugby and my culture and things about myself that I know.

We then worked together as a CIT to discuss what the data suggested in terms of the direction for our next inquiry. We decided that analysis of all the data suggested that the second inquiry should address a "What happens if …?" practitioner research question, focused on writing in the senior school. Hence, the questions for the next inquiry were:

- What happens if we change our approach to writing in the senior school in terms of student engagement and enjoyment in writing?
- What, if any, effect will this have on students being sent out of class because of challenging behaviour?

To prepare for the inquiry, we talked as a CIT and consulted an external language expert about ways to increase student engagement and enjoyment in writing. Our discussions confirmed the importance of experiential learning as a way of increasing students' motivation to write. We then worked with a teacher from the senior school who volunteered to do a 4-week trial of a language-experience approach to writing. In contrast to our usual approach, where teachers specified the genre for writing, we introduced a language stimulus (in this case, a worm farm) and invited the children to choose the genre they wanted to use. We worked with the teacher in a critical-friend role to implement and assess the impact of this new approach. An analysis of the children's writing outputs showed that all children completed some form of writing (which had not been the case previously). The teacher noted that the language-experience approach supported everyone to write, even the reluctant ones who often struggled with getting their ideas down on paper. Interview data from children showed that they really liked being able to choose a genre rather than being told to write in a specified genre. During the trial period no children were sent out of class for challenging behaviour during writing time.

The outcomes from the inquiry indicated that a language-experience approach to writing could reduce classroom inequities by providing opportunities for all the children to be successful writers. The approach also improved equity by reducing interruptions and loss of time through children being sent out of class. The teacher commented, "The worms gave a everyone a much richer experience in terms of language, motivation, and outcomes." The results of the inquiry prompted deep discussions with the principal and other staff about what would be an effective writing programme for our school, and how we would go about introducing a different approach across the school in the future.

## *What we learnt from undertaking inquiries as a cross-school CIT*

The key thing we learnt was the power of working collaboratively with colleagues from different contexts. Collaborating with someone in a similar role from a different school supported us as senior leaders to dig deeper into our inquiries as we brought our combined professional expertise to bear on each of our school-focused problems of practice. Similarly, working with the university teacher educator was critical in supporting us to use inquiry as a structured research process. The probing questions that were asked and the encouragement to go back to the data to check our assumptions rather than jumping to conclusions supported us to engage in systematic data analysis and goal setting. It was refreshing to work with people from outside the school. When you are in the midst of the situation you can't always see what is really going on. Having "outsiders" looking in and bringing different viewpoints and ideas to our discussions certainly helped us see the bigger picture as well as deepen our professional thinking and research expertise.

We also learnt a lot more about equity. Although we and our schools had a strong commitment to diversity and social justice, undertaking equity-linked inquiries as a CIT challenged the way we thought about equity and the impact it had on our learners. Working in a cross-school CIT opened up our practice to scrutiny from different perspectives. We believed that our systems and processes were promoting equity in our schools, but when we gathered data about what was happening, we discovered there were unintended consequences. Incidents of challenging behaviour were not just about the behaviour or the students, but about classroom programmes, expectations, and understanding our learners' experiences.

While the Facets of Practice for Equity were a useful tool to focus our inquiries, they also proved to be an effective framework to consider and address inequities in our schools. Through our CIT discussions, we grew our understandings of why things work or don't work in different contexts, and how being equity-focused means taking an inquiry stance to our work as teachers and leaders. Although Facet 6:

*Recognising and seeking to address classroom, school and societal practices that reproduce inequity* was the focus for our research, in reality our inquiries addressed all the Facets. We learnt that to bring about systemic change we need to take account of all six Facets.

Working as a cross-school CIT also helped us to maintain momentum with our inquiries. Given the demands of schools, especially on senior leaders, it is easy for urgent problems to overtake good intentions. Working collaboratively with outsiders in a specific time frame helped us to prioritise our inquiries. The fact that we were senior staff and did not have our own classes was important because it meant we had flexibility to undertake our inquiries and meet as a CIT. This freedom allowed us to forward plan our CIT meetings and this gave us time-frames and targets for our research. The trusting relationships we developed as members of the CIT also helped us keep going. Undertaking our inquiries sometimes involved dealing with complex situations involving colleagues, so it was vital that we could discuss things openly and honestly in a safe environment. Being able to bounce ideas off each other confidentially, and knowing that members of the team were there to support and encourage us, helped our inquiries to keep moving forward.

# Chapter 6
# Principals' perspectives on the project

A recent Education Review Office report (ERO, 2016b) reiterates the key role that effective leadership plays in establishing the conditions for improving student outcomes. As the report states, "Leadership that works matters in education" (p. 5). This was certainly true of the Teaching and Learning Research Initiative (TLRI) project that informed this book.[15] The presence of principals as contributors in our Collaborative Inquiry Community (CIC) meant that they could see and appreciate the work that was happening, offer resources and ideas to support the work, and align the work with the "big picture" of their schools' goals and direction. The two principals' contributions sent a strong message that the work was valuable and important. Their participation also provided an opportunity for them to hear about their staff's beliefs and ideas, and to work with colleagues in another school to test out ideas and assumptions. Our experience in the TLRI project adds weight to other research findings (e.g., Robinson, Hohepa, &

---

15 "Teaching for Equity: How do we do it?" was a 2-year project funded by the Teaching and Learning Research Initiative. The final report for the project is available from the TLRI website http://www.tlri.org.nz/tlri-research/research-completed/cross-sector/teaching-equity-how-do-we-do-it.

Lloyd, 2009) that engagement of school leadership in teachers' collaborative work has positive outcomes for teachers and students.

This chapter focuses on the principals' perspectives on their schools' involvement in the project. In particular, it looks at what they perceived to be the benefits and challenges of being part of a cross-sector CIC. A thematic analysis of individual interviews with the two principals identified three major themes:

1. creating connections to improve practice
2. building capacity
3. teacher inquiry and research.

These themes are discussed in the following sections of this chapter.

## Creating connections to improve practice

For both principals, a key benefit of the project was the collaboration between the two schools and the university. As one of the principals put it, "The opportunity to work with another school, particularly a school out of our area, and not necessarily in the same kind of context or community, added another dimension." The principals thought that the added dimension related to the following points:

- Working with another school gave them a chance to compare how they were enacting school and classroom practices to promote equity: "You get a bit of a yardstick about what you're doing and how effective that might be when you can pop it up there against what someone else is doing."

- The project provided a framework that allowed the principals to step outside the everyday busyness of their professional lives. One thought that "When you are focused on your own environment, you don't question as much as you would when other people are looking and asking you to critique your practice and you have the opportunity to do the same with them."

- Opening up their practice to scrutiny was seen as a learning opportunity. Both principals enjoyed being able to share ideas and discuss why they took a particular approach to a problem of practice. They thought that having project team meetings in each other's school was a benefit, as being on site helped trigger conversations around particular approaches to promoting equity. Observing specific practices for equity in the other school stimulated questioning and analysis.

Working with the university, as well as with another school, was identified as being another benefit, with one principal saying they "really enjoyed sharing expertise across the two educational landscapes". While both schools had been working on enhancing equitable student outcomes for some time, they thought that the TLRI project provided:

> … a good opportunity to work with colleagues from the university who had the skills and knowledge to critique what we were doing and provide input and guidance on where we were heading, what we had achieved in the past, and what our next steps might be.

The principals acknowledged that connections developed between the schools and between the schools and the university contributed to capacity building for all team members.

## *Building capacity*

While both principals had a long-time commitment to teacher professional learning and development, they thought that engagement in the TLRI project provided particular benefits for them, and the teachers, in the following ways.

- For the principals, it was an opportunity to support the participating teachers to build their knowledge, skills, and confidence in work important to the schools. One commented that "The added bonus was being able to really engage with a small number of our own staff who we thought could take the next step up."

- The principals also learnt from each other.

  > It was really interesting to see how other principals go about doing things … and the different ways to build up teachers' knowledge and understandings. There were things that we learnt to do and things we learnt not to do and things that [we realised] would not work for our kids.

- Principals liked the way the cross-school approach enabled people to "get out and see people in other settings," and thought this,

along with the discussions, provided enhanced opportunities for teacher professional learning.
- Being involved in the research aspects of the project was also seen to be "really valuable". The principals appreciated how their teachers' research skills and knowledge had been well developed. They thought that presenting at an educational research conference during the project was a real positive because it "enhanced the teachers' mana as leaders and as practitioner researchers".

## *Teacher inquiry and research*

Both schools used teacher inquiry prior to the TLRI project. While they thought that the project "reinforced what we did anyway", their experiences confirmed the importance of teacher inquiry and its power for supporting teacher self-reflection for action. One principal said, "It really made me realise how important it is—how it's a practical, sensible, and manageable way of refining practice and creating improvement." Additionally, the principals also noted that the project's specific focus on inquiry as a research process "added another layer of refinement [to teacher inquiry] which was really valuable". The research approach ensured that the inquiries were "purposeful, systematic and coherent … [they] made things happen". In this regard, one principal commented on the research leadership provided by the university members of the CIC to the inquiry; the university team members "were able to guide the participants in the research thoughtfully and carefully".

## *Concluding thoughts*

While both principals identified a number of benefits regarding their own and their schools' experience in the TLRI project, they did not identify any major challenges. Perhaps this was because of the resourcing made available through the TLRI. As discussed previously, the funding made it possible to pay for teachers to be released to engage in the project team meetings. One principal commented on the essential role of resourcing:

> Resourcing was essential. When you are resourced well you can support people properly and it can become part of what they do rather than an extra. People can resent it when they use their time to produce things for other people.

The principals also stressed how the trust that developed through "non-threatening and collaborative" engagement in the CIC over the 2 years of the TLRI played a key role in the project. Trust was the key to empowering everyone to honestly engage in deep discussion and critique "without feeling that people were making judgements on what someone else was doing". They recognised the strength that comes from openly sharing practice. Everyone contributed and was a leader, no matter what their status or position in the school. One principal put it this way:

> The key to improvement in schools is that people collaborate rather than compete. We have commonalities we can share with each other and yet each setting is unique and distinct. And that is important to recognise because with any project you want people to feel safe when they are participating … because there was high trust, people felt safe.

The principals' engagement in professional learning alongside the teachers and teacher educators was very powerful because it validated the work being undertaken and modelled a non-hierarchical approach to collaborative knowledge-building.

It should also be noted that the deputy principals (DPs) played a significant role in the TLRI project. Their participation was helped by the fact that they were not classroom-based DPs. Being "walking DPs" (without their own classes) meant they could allocate "work" time—as opposed to outside-of-the-classroom time—to the project. The work of the CIC and CITs became an integral part their leadership roles rather than being an add-on to a classroom teacher's role. These senior leaders acted as brokers, organising resources for the work—such as release time and spaces—and acting as communication points between school and university team members. The commitment of the DPs turned the talk of the meetings into action. In this TLRI project the DPs were also able to work together, across the two schools, providing support and challenging each other as they undertook the same role in different contexts. The DPs' experiences of working together as a CIT are explored in Chapter 5.

# Chapter 7
# Enhancing equity through inquiry: Key findings

Although the Teaching and Learning Research Initiative (TLRI) project described in this book was undertaken with participants from one university and two primary schools, it points a way towards increasing equitable education across Aotearoa New Zealand's diverse schooling context.[16] The project demonstrated practitioners' commitment to changing their practice through engagement in knowledge building based on an evidence-based framework of teaching for equity (Grudnoff et al., 2017) and an inquiry approach. Although the project was exploratory in nature, it demonstrated that, with resources and a commitment to work together, teachers, principals, and university teacher educators can make changes to promote equity in both school systems and classrooms.

## *Collaborative inquiry for equity*

In this final chapter, we pull together the key findings from both phases of the 2-year project and discuss the possibilities of collaborative

---

16 "Teaching for Equity: How do we do it?" was a 2-year project funded by the Teaching and Learning Research Initiative. The final report for the project is available from the TLRI website http://www.tlri.org.nz/tlri-research/research-completed/cross-sector/teaching-equity-how-do-we-do-it?

inquiry, guided by a conceptual framework, to increase equity in our classrooms. Our work indicates that sharing a set of principles for teaching for equity and approaching inquiry in a collaborative manner were crucial to changing practice in the schools involved. As a result of analysing our findings across both phases of the project, we have identified eight features of the collaborative inquiry approach that led to this change. These are summarised in Table 7.1 along with brief examples from the project. Each feature is then discussed, drawing from the examples presented in the book as well as from other studies of collaborative inquiry. We suggest that considering these eight features might be helpful for others engaged in collaborative inquiry work.

Table 7.1 **Eight features of successful collaborative inquiry to increase equity**

| Feature of collaborative inquiry | Brief description | Examples from the project |
|---|---|---|
| 1. Integrating expertise | Collaborators from different institutions and with different expertise challenge taken-for-granted approaches and increase the inquiry capability of the team. Engaging external experts, including those with indigenous and cultural knowledge, also supports knowledge building and use. | The research expertise of the university teacher educators, coupled with the practice expertise of the teachers and leaders from two different school contexts, was harnessed to bring about new ways of working for equity in classrooms. A leading international scholar, Professor Marilyn Cochran-Smith, provided fresh perspectives to inquiry approaches, challenged accepted notions of teacher inquiry, and motivated the Collaborative Inquiry Teams (CITs) to investigate strategies that could address inequitable practices. |
| 2. Building trust | In order to investigate sensitive issues in colleagues' classrooms, it is necessary to build trust so that collaboration can thrive. This is particularly the case where teams are drawn from across an employment hierarchy and/or from differing cultural backgrounds. | We built trust slowly over time, beginning with sometimes quite long Phase 1 Collaborative Inquiry Community (CIC) meetings to discuss and examine each of the Facets of Practice for Equity (Facets) in detail. We scheduled extended meetings to investigate how theory and practice could help us develop a deep understanding of each Facet. We included university, school leadership, and classroom teachers on every occasion to provide the conditions for trust to develop. |

| Feature of collaborative inquiry | Brief description | Examples from the project |
| --- | --- | --- |
| 3. Working together as a diverse team | Diversity in team membership in terms of experience, role, culture, and other factors promotes problem recognition and innovative resolution. | The collaborative teams included university and school members from a range of cultures and experiences. As a result, a diverse range of issues such as family interactions and accessibility were raised and addressed through various new strategies. |
| 4. Including inquiry-minded leadership | Collaborative inquiry requires supportive professional and research leadership. | University teacher educators provided the inquiry leadership. They worked in partnership with school leaders to provide the conditions necessary for teachers to implement projects at the classroom level, where change happens. |
| 5. Resourcing inquiry | Collaborative inquiry requires sufficient resourcing to enable the collaboration/s to function without overburdening those involved. | Funding from the TLRI enabled teacher release from classroom duties. The senior leaders at each school also contributed and organised resources so that the CIC and CITs could function effectively. These resources included additional teacher release time, IT systems, meeting rooms, timetabling, and other organisational matters. |
| 6. Incorporating inquiry as both stance and project | Different techniques are required for different purposes. They depend on where the inquiry takes place, and what the problem for investigation is. | The CIC aimed to enrich and extend the Facets and thus used collaborative knowledge building, whereas the CITs aimed to use the Facets to find ways to teach for more equitable outcomes for students. |
| 7. Using data | Gathering and analysing data in systematic ways enables the team to learn from, and use, the findings. | The inquiries were informed by a formal inquiry process grounded in posing a research question, collecting and analysing data, exploring evidence, and testing out new approaches in further spirals of inquiry. |
| 8. Incorporating conceptual frameworks | Capturing the important ideas in a way that is easy to remember and apply provides a shared frame of reference to guide inquiry. | The six Facets of Practice for Equity provided focus for discussion and analysis, for inquiry, and for co-construction of the meaning of equity and its implications for practice. |

## 1. Integrating expertise to generate collaborative inquiry

As the chapters in this book demonstrate, each of the members involved in our collaborative inquiries brought a different set of expertise to the projects. In the CIC, spanning both years of the study, the university teacher-educator members provided the springboard for investigating how to teach for equity, through utilising the Facets framework and integrating research expertise from Māori and Western worlds. As Earl and Timperley (2008) remind us, "Innovative solutions arise when people in groups draw on evidence and outside explicit knowledge and combine it with tacit knowledge in response to authentic problems" (p. 2). In Phase 1, Year 1, we consciously implemented professional learning conversations to provide the basis for evidence-informed educational improvement, most specifically to produce more equitable outcomes. While scholars (e.g., Conner, 2015; Jesson, Wilson, McNaughton, & Lai, 2017; Sinnema, Alansari, & Turner, 2018) have identified conditions underpinning effective collaborative inquiry for improvement, relatively little attention has been given to the point that for collaborations to be fully effective and achieve new or different outcomes, different kinds of expertise are necessary. Our approach deliberately and sometimes fortuitously involved collaborators with different types of expertise and from different cultural and educational contexts. One of the university teacher-educator CIC members provided a Māori cultural perspective that raised questions about the relevance of teaching approaches and resources for some students; some team members brought expertise in gifted and special education that helped us challenge taken-for-granted ways of teaching; others raised equity issues from a spectrum of perspectives that made us re-evaluate what the implementation of the Facets might look like in Aotearoa New Zealand's very diverse schools and classrooms.

In addition to the diversity of expertise we drew upon in our CIC, we also invited a leading international scholar in the field of teacher inquiry to work intensively with the CIC team for one entire day when we were planning our Phase 2 inquiry projects. Professor Marilyn Cochran-Smith workshopped our collaborative team inquiry planning with us, extending our understanding of inquiry as stance (Cochran-Smith & Lytle, 2009), and challenged us to see our collaborative work as both theoretically informed and practical in effect. The need for such external expertise to accelerate and strengthen collaborative professional learning has been confirmed in many studies (e.g., Cordingley, 2015; Hill, 2016; Lai & McNaughton, 2008; Timperley, Wilson, Barrar, &

Fung, 2007), and its influence was confirmed in our project. As well as learning from Cochran-Smith's experience and the workshop activities that helped the CIC to raise issues and plan investigations to address them, the experience of working with an external expert contributed to our knowledge building and to the cohesiveness of the team.

## 2. Building trust across a collaborative inquiry community

A second key factor in building knowledge about the Facets and how to put them into practice in the classroom was the consistent focus on their use, through long face-to-face meetings of teachers, teacher educators, and school leaders. As described in Chapter 2, in Phase 1 the team met five times at each school and twice as a full CIC. Most of the meetings lasted for at least 3 hours, with a total of almost 50 hours. The transcript analysis of practitioners' and teacher educators' discussions about what the Facets might look like in practice identified a number of conversational knowledge-building processes:

- presenting (sharing)
- clarifying (inviting comment)
- adding (providing more information or an additional example)
- querying (seeking additional information, sometimes of practice, sometimes contextual)
- reflecting
- theorising practice
- considering implications (for individual child, class group, teacher, school, parents and whānau)
- summarising (and/or affirming).

Through these conversational processes the CIC achieved the aim of building and sharing knowledge about practices for equity. At the same time, and perhaps more importantly, these processes provided the multi-dimensional interconnections that built trust in our working relationships.

Although we used both face-to-face meetings and online tools to collaborate, our analysis of the face-to-face discussions indicates that we built relational trust through the types of conversations that took place. Robinson, Hohepa, and Lloyd (2009) describe the importance of relational trust:

> Trust is critical in contexts where the success of one person's efforts is dependent on the contribution of others ... Relational trust involves a willingness to be vulnerable because one has confidence that others will play their part. It should not be mistaken for feelings of warmth or affection. (p. 183)

Relational trust is foundational in learning communities where significant impacts have been demonstrated in terms of student learning outcomes (Bryk, 2010). Labelled as both the "connective tissue" of effective education (Bryk & Schneider, 2003) and the "glue" of professional learning communities (Cranston, 2011), trust is essential if the type of change needed to bring about equity of outcomes is to occur. Relational trust fosters collaboration and promotes "willingness among staff to grow professionally" (Cranston, 2011, p. 59).

Since relational trust is a social process and is "grounded in the social respect that comes from the kinds of social discourse that take place across a school community" (Bryk & Schneider, 2003, p. 41), we examined the kinds of conversation we engaged in during our Phase 1 knowledge-building meetings to understand how we had built relational trust. We found that our conversational strategies aligned closely with those required for building a high sense of trust. Glaser's (2013) conversational intelligence matrix supports our finding that our face-to-face meetings nurtured rich and constructive conversations that were successful because they built the trust needed to collaborate. Glaser's matrix provides an explanation of the levels of conversation humans engage in. At the lowest level (transactional), we give and take information but mostly focus on what we, as individuals, can take from the conversation. This level of conversation is "I" focused and involves only low levels of trust. At the second level (positional), we explore others' positions to achieve a win–win solution. At this level, we advocate and inquire, with a focus on both "I" and "we" as we negotiate outcomes to achieve our goals, building conditional trust. However, to develop the trustful relationships needed to achieve mutual success, conversations need to become transformational (the third level). These are the kind of conversations that developed in our project. In our team conversations, we collaborated by sharing and discovering insights about equity in teaching and learning, by exploring other people's perspectives, and by joining with others to transform reality, co-create, and innovate.

Through transformational conversational strategies, the CIC extended as well as confirmed the original conception of the Facets and built a common understanding of what they might mean in practice. Our professional inquiry conversations enabled us to elaborate and exemplify the Facets for each other. There was another important outcome of this process: while the Facets were defined as six indicators of teaching for equity, in discussing how they worked in practice we could see that they were very much integrated and intricately linked. For example, explanations of Facet 1: *Selecting worthwhile content and designing and implementing learning opportunities aligned to valued learning outcomes*, were often linked to Facet 2: *Connecting to students as learners, and to their lives and experiences*; Facet 3: *Creating learning-focused, respectful and supportive learning environments*; and Facet 4: *Using evidence to scaffold learning and improve teaching*. We also found that Facet 6: *Recognising and seeking to address classroom, school and societal practices that reproduce inequity*, was integral to the other five Facets. This finding is consistent with the theoretical conceptualisation of the Facets as general principles, recognising the complexity of teaching and learning, rather than as specific strategies or behaviours (Cochran-Smith et al., 2014).

### 3. Working together as a diverse team

As noted in Chapter 2, conversations with only like-minded people rarely lead to assumptions being challenged and new ideas developed. Diverse teams can challenge members' ideas and assumptions. The differences presented in a diverse team can lead to more knowledge-building, as the act of trying to deeply understand each other provides potential for professional learning and growth. As previously noted, our team was diverse in terms of experience, role, culture, and other factors, and we discovered that this diversity promoted both problem recognition and innovative solutions. By building trust over time and through professional inquiry conversations, we became able to challenge each other and problematise existing embedded practices that, with careful examination, could be seen as barriers to equity.

As shown above, discussions of any one of the Facets regularly included links to Facet 6, highlighting how the notions captured by Facet 6 underpinned the practices of the teachers in the study. At one school, a discussion of Facet 1: *Selecting worthwhile content and designing and implementing learning opportunities aligned to valued learning outcomes* exemplified this. During this discussion, teachers explored how to support a student with severe physical disabilities on a nature-study trip to an offshore island. The trip involved transfers from bus to boat and from boat to island wharf as well as movement along pathways once on the island. Originally, the school thought that the student would be better left at school because of difficulties managing the trip in her wheelchair. However, following our discussions on equity, the teachers planning the trip worked with the school's special needs co-ordinator to investigate how the student could take part in this learning opportunity. Understanding that she would need to be provided with additional assistance, the school contacted the island's caretakers and rangers to organise mobility support so that the student could move around the island with her peers. The teachers believed that this solution arose because they had come to consider equity more carefully. Our collaborative inquiry discussions enabled members of the group to bring forward different perspectives, and extend understanding of how the concept of equity differs from that of equality. In summary, working in trusting relationships within a diverse group resulted in new and challenging ideas that led the teachers to move their practice towards more equitable approaches.

## 4. Including inquiry-minded leadership

It became clear that leadership supportive of inquiry, and knowledgeable about the Facets, was a critical feature of our collaborative inquiry venture. By leadership, we mean both school and project leadership. From the beginning of the TLRI project, the principals of both schools ensured that it ran smoothly, engaged in the collaborative discussions, and contributed in many ways that facilitated engagement with the project. As explored in Chapter 6, the principals were fully on board with the purpose of the project and actively encouraged the participation of teachers in their schools. The DPs, too, were a factor in the success of the inquiry aspects of the project. In concert with their principals, they ensured relief teachers were employed to release others for inquiry meetings, communicated with the university teacher-educator team members to co-ordinate meetings, and worked across contexts to build strong relationships that underpinned the cross-school inquiry projects.

The principals and DPs in this project exhibited all five leadership dimensions that have been identified as having direct and indirect effects on improving student outcomes (Robinson, Hohepa, & Lloyd, 2009). They actively engaged in three of these dimensions in relation to the project. These leaders worked with the university teacher educators to establish goals and expectations, and they knew about and understood the Facet framework as a guiding force for setting these goals and expectations. They resourced the project in ways that strategically enabled and encouraged engagement, and, in particular, they promoted and encouraged their teachers to participate in the project for their professional learning and development.

University teacher educators also provided leadership in the project. They worked in partnership with the principals and their deputies to provide the conditions necessary for teachers to implement projects at the classroom level, where change happens. Feedback from the teachers and school leaders indicated that although they had engaged in school-based inquiry prior to the TLRI project, having external support motivated the CITs to pursue and complete their inquiries, systematically collect and analyse data, and share the findings publicly at conferences and through publications.

## 5. Supporting inquiry through resourcing

Funding from the TLRI enabled release from classroom responsibilities so that teachers could focus on our collaborative inquiry discussions, and, in Phase 2, meet with university team members to work on planning, data analysis, and dissemination activities. The leadership at the university level and in each school organised resources so that the collaborations could function well, through such aspects as IT systems, meeting rooms, timetabling, and other measures. Although teaching as inquiry is seen as part of teachers' daily work, extra resourcing for teacher release, hospitality, and travel to attend conferences and share findings with others helps to build inquiry team cohesion and underscores the importance of the work.

Having university team members in the inquiry teams was another aspect of resourcing that helped the CITs complete successful inquiries and learn more about increasing equity. The teacher educators were resourced through the TLRI funding and brought with them research and facilitation skills that supported and extended the teachers' inquiry capabilities. Expertise-related resources are critical to professional learning, providing the stretch to extend thinking and practice. In particular, the teacher educators provided stretch through research evidence and expertise, which supported CIT inquiry planning, analysis, and implementation. Combined with the professional expertise from the schools, these forms of expertise are significant contributors to professional learning and development (Cordingley, 2015). As discussed in Chapter 5, this project provides evidence that having research expertise in the team is important to the success of collaborative inquiries.

## 6. Incorporating inquiry as both stance and project

For insightful inquiry to take place, different techniques are required for different purposes, depending on where the inquiry takes place and what the problem for investigation is. In this project, the entire CIC was interested in and committed to a two-pronged focus. First, throughout the project, we were working on elaborating, refining, and modifying the Facets framework as a guiding set of principles. Secondly, we were using the Facets framework to drive the classroom and school inquiries in order to produce more equitable outcomes for students. Both aspects informed each other and provided frames of reference that kept us grounded in what we were trying to achieve. Put another way, the CIC, which spanned the full duration of the project, aimed to enrich and extend the Facets and thus used a collaborative knowledge-building approach. In contrast, the CITs aimed to use the Facets we were building knowledge about to find ways to teach for more equitable outcomes for students. Both these aims fed into each other as the project proceeded, enriching our inquiry stance.

As a result of the CIT inquiries, the project team built deep knowledge about how the Facets could (and did) guide decision-making in teachers' professional practice. And, as explained in Chapter 2, Facet 2 was adapted following the knowledge-building phase of the project to include specific reference to students' learning in addition to connecting with their lives and experiences. During the CIT projects in Phase 2, teachers focused more closely on consciously making these connections and using their knowledge about students' lives and experiences to make their lessons more relevant to build student learning. In the process, our understandings about Facet 2 continued to increase and deepen.

## 7. Grounding inquiry through data collection and analysis

Working in CITs that included both research and professional expertise facilitated a strong focus on systematic data collection and analysis. This was important to the success of the inquiry process. As explored in depth in an evaluation of the Teacher-led Innovation Fund (TLIF) (Sinnema et al., 2018), even when teachers are willing to lead and engage in inquiry projects, issues with data capability are widespread: "Teachers report a lack of confidence and skill and that is evident in the quality of the data collected and analysis" (Sinnema et al., 2018, p. 14). Having combined expertise from researchers and practising teachers deepened and strengthened data capability in our project.

The data in Phase 1 were the ideas and experiences of the teachers and leaders related to each Facet of the conceptual framework. As explained in Chapter 2, these were produced through the professional inquiry conversations held throughout the first year of the project. Through participating in the discussions and recording and exploring the ideas shared, the CIC came to new understandings of how the Facets might be used to shift practice within classrooms. Chapters 3, 4, and 5 provide rich examples of how data were collected and collaboratively analysed, and how the Facets were used to shape CIT inquiries. Careful data analysis and sharing research results at an Aotearoa New Zealand education conference were new experiences for the teachers. The teacher educators' research expertise in the CITs supported the teachers to develop expertise, confidence, and know-how to take their inquiry through the full research life cycle, culminating in public sharing.

Although teaching as inquiry is a central pillar of *The New Zealand Curriculum* (Ministry of Education, 2007), inquiry as stance is a broader and deeper conception requiring a continuous inquiry mindset and the research knowledge and skills to investigate professional practice systematically. Each of the CIT investigations was more than sharing examples and ideas. We actively engaged in systematic, intentional, and iterative inquiry (Grudnoff, Haigh, Jackson, & Passfield, 2018). That is, for each CIT there were sustained cyclical rounds of critical discussion with an external expert about the implications for learners, followed by carefully planned interventions, data collection, and analysis (Cochran-Smith & Lytle, 2009; Cordingley, 2015). The teachers within the CITs were clear that they had learnt to "learn from looking through exploration of evidence about pupil outcomes and from observing teaching and learning exchanges especially those involving experiments with new approaches" (Cordingley, 2015, p. 240). Using a rigorous, systematic approach, the teachers stated that they had needed to constantly go back to their data, question their original assumptions and, as a result, come to different conclusions and suggestions for change. This process was motivated by teachers' and leaders' aspirations to increase equitable outcomes for their students, and the Facets of Practice for Equity (Grudnoff et al., 2017) steered us forward with aspirations for students as a central intention (Timperley et al., 2007).

## 8. Using a conceptual framework to stimulate and organise collaborative inquiry

Using a conceptual framework provided a focus for the collaborative inquiry project. As in any research project, a conceptual frame for inquiry guides the entire process by giving a framework to build ideas on, or by providing an explanation of concepts in a way that is easy to remember and apply. Cordingley's (2015) factors for successfully continuing professional development include aspirations for students to succeed and the role of theory. Our key conceptual framework, the Facets of Practice for Equity, was theoretically derived and based on international evidence, but this project aimed to test its feasibility and practicality. We used this framework as our focus of interest. We examined what each of the Facets might add to teachers' understanding and practice, but, at the same time, the team members looked for what might be missing from the framework, and how it might be further developed in and for the Aotearoa New Zealand primary school context.

Our conceptual framework kept us focused on our goal of shifting teaching practices towards more equitable outcomes for students. The frame provided a way forward. By examining each of the Facets individually and in connection with each other, we were able to build banks of ideas that could inform teaching and, simultaneously, remind us to ask how we were seeking to address barriers to equity in each context. In our CIC and CITs, we used the equity focus to figure out "why things do and don't work in different contexts to develop an underpinning rationale or practical theory alongside practice" (Cordingley, 2015, p. 241).

Our focused inquiry in both phases of the project also fed back into sharpening and contextualising the framework for use in Aotearoa New Zealand schools. Although the Facets of Practice for Equity were drawn from Aotearoa New Zealand best evidence syntheses (Aitken & Sinnema, 2008; Anthony & Walshaw, 2007; Timperley et al., 2007) and the Te Kotahitanga project (Bishop, Berryman, & Wearmouth, 2014), they also drew on international programmes of research and thus were general in their focus. Throughout our 2-year project we were constantly asking questions about the relevance of the framework for the Aotearoa New Zealand context, specifically in the primary school sector. As the chapters in this book demonstrate, the Facets provided principles that guided professional inquiry and practice. With important modifications to Facet 2 and Facet 6, the framework sustained our focus on equity and assisted the CITs to push forward on the equity agenda by making practical changes to teaching and school programmes. We include Table 7.2 below on the assumption that it may provide a useful conceptual framework for professional practice and inquiry in classroom and school settings.

Table 7.2 **Facets of Practice for Equity**

| | |
|---|---|
| Facet 1 | Selecting worthwhile content and designing and implementing learning opportunities aligned to valued learning outcomes |
| Facet 2 | Connecting to students as learners, and to their lives and experiences |
| Facet 3 | Creating learning-focused, respectful and supportive learning environments |
| Facet 4 | Using evidence to scaffold learning and improve teaching |
| Facet 5 | Adopting an inquiry stance and taking responsibility for further professional engagement and learning |
| Facet 6 | Recognising and seeking to address classroom, school and societal practices that reproduce inequity |

In summary, the eight features described in this chapter enabled us to work as a CIC to push towards more equitable outcomes for students in these two primary schools. While these features align strongly with Cordingley's framework for effective professional development, which draws on two Aotearoa New Zealand best evidence syntheses (Robinson et al., 2009; Timperley et al., 2007), they also move beyond this to demonstrate the importance of relational trust, emotional engagement, and a guiding theoretical framework.

## *Implications and possibilities for collaborative inquiry*

This project has implications and suggests possibilities for increasing the rigour of collaborative inquiry in schools. It also confirms that making a difference to the educational outcomes of students, particularly those most at risk of underachievement, is not straightforward and will not be achieved through teaching inquiry pursued pro forma for compliance with school policies or performance management. Our project demonstrated that teaching for equity requires sustained focus on how equitable outcomes might be achieved, that is with the guidance of the Facets and through the sustained agentic action of the school working as an inquiry community. To conclude we summarise below what we learnt about engaging in collaborative inquiry to enhance teaching for equity.

1. **The value of cross-sector collaborative inquiry communities.** Our project demonstrated the value of working in cross-sector collaborative inquiry communities. Our CIC and CITs included both pedagogical and research expertise, providing rich opportunities for building knowledge and skills for equitable teaching practices. Bringing together practitioners with university teacher-educator researchers encouraged and supported stretch for all team members and challenged us to do better for all students in these schools.

2. **The importance of identifying and challenging classroom and school practices that marginalise learners and their parents/caregivers.** Teaching for equity requires practitioners to identify and challenge classroom and school practices that

marginalise learners and their parents/caregivers. Through our investigations we learnt that deep understanding of the difference between equity and equality in relation to teaching and learning is critical. Without such an understanding, changes may remain superficial, and student outcomes mostly remain unchanged.

3. **The power of inquiry as a process for investigating and changing practice.** While inquiry can lead to teaching for equity, collecting systematic evidence from practice and rigorous analysis require an investment of time and expertise. It is necessary to think about what to collect and how to collect it, and to work out what the data means for enhancing teaching and learning.

4. **The crucial contribution of resourcing.** Having support, encouragement, and the time and space to work collaboratively outside of the everyday business of teaching and classrooms is vital to building, sharing, and implementing practical knowledge for teaching for equity. Even with the very best willpower, busy teachers and leaders find it difficult to find the space for the time-consuming work of systematic collaborative investigation and intervention without supportive leadership and the resources of time and expertise.

5. **The importance of building trust.** Teachers and leaders need to feel safe to identify and honestly discuss issues arising from their inquiries and their learning. Working together over time on real problems of practice, with the support of critically engaged colleagues and honest collaborative inquiry discussions, builds trust. Accountability measures must be carefully designed to support inquiry that leads to systematic improvements for equity.

6. **The importance of communal knowledge-building.** In this project, we explored face-to-face as well online approaches. We included electronic means in the hope that we could demonstrate how networked communities might build knowledge together online. We discovered that while web-based systems can be used to build and share professional knowledge,

stability and access issues must be addressed for this to be effective. Our findings strongly suggest that web-based systems need to be supplemented with face-to-face engagement in order to build trust and facilitate rich discussion and learning within a collaborative inquiry community.

# References

Aitken, G., & Sinnema, C. (2008). *Effective pedagogy in social sciences / tikanga ā-iwi. Best evidence synthesis iteration (BES)*. Wellington: Ministry of Education.

Alton-Lee, A. (2003). *Quality teaching for diverse students in schooling: Best evidence synthesis iteration (BES)*. Wellington: Ministry of Education.

Anthony, G., & Walshaw, M. (2007). *Effective pedagogy in mathematics/pāngarau: Best evidence synthesis iteration (BES)*. Wellington: Ministry of Education.

Anthony, G., & Walshaw, M. (2009). *Effective pedagogy in mathematics*. International Academy of Education. Retrieved from http://www.ibe.unesco.org/fileadmin/user_upload/Publications/Educational_Practices/EdPractices_19.pdf

Babione, C. (2014). *Practitioner teacher inquiry and research*. New York, NY: Jossey-Bass.

Bishop, R., & Berryman, M. (2006). *Culture speaks: Cultural relationships and classroom learning*. Wellington: Huia.

Bishop, R., & Berryman, M. (2009). The Te Kotahitanga effective teaching profile. *Set: Research Information for Teachers, 2*, 5–11.

Bishop, R., Berryman, M., & Wearmouth, J. (2014). *Te Kotahitanga: Towards effective education reform for indigenous and other minority students*. Wellington: NZCER Press.

Berryman, M., Pennicott, K., & Tiatia, S. (2018). Te puna wai ora, e tu atu nei e: Stand up, stand strong and be proud. In E. McKinley & L. Smith (Eds.), *Handbook of indigenous education* (pp. 1–25). Singapore: Springer. http://dx.doi.org/10.1007/978-981-10-1839-8_53-1

Bryk, A. S. (2010). Organising schools for improvement. *Phi Delta Kappan, 91*(7), 23–30. doi.org/10.1177/003172171009100705

Bryk, A. S., & Schneider, B. (2003). Trust in schools: A core resource for school reform. *Educational Leadership, 60*(6), 40–45.

Chapin, S., O'Connor, C., & Anderson, N. (2013). *Talk moves* (3rd ed.). Sausalito, CA: Maths Solutions.

Cochran-Smith, M., Ell, F., Grudnoff, L., Ludlow L., Haigh M., & Hill, M. (2014, Winter). When complexity theory meets critical realism: A platform for research on initial teacher education. *Teacher Education Quarterly, 41*(1), 105–122.

Cochran-Smith, M., & Lytle, S. L. (2009). *Inquiry as stance: Practitioner research for the next generation.* New York, NY: Teachers College Press.

Conner, L. (2015). *Teaching as inquiry with a focus on priority learners.* Wellington: NZCER Press.

Cordingley, P. (2015). The contribution of research to teachers' professional learning and development. *Oxford Review of Education, 41*(2), 234–252. http://dx.doi.org/10.1080/03054985.2015.1020105

Cranston, J. (2011). Relational trust: The glue that binds a professional learning community. *Journal of Educational Research, 57*(1), 59–72.

Dalton, S. S. (2007). *Five standards for effective teaching: How to succeed with all learners, grades K–8.* San Francisco, CA: Wiley.

Earl, L. M., & Timperley, H.(2008). *Professional learning conversations: Challenges in using evidence for improvement.* London, UK: Springer.

Education Council New Zealand | Matatū Aotearoa. (2011). *Tātaiako cultural competencies for teachers of Māori learners.* Wellington: Ministry of Education. Retrieved from https://www.educationcouncil.org.nz/content/t%C4%81taiako-cultural-competencies-teachers-m%C4%81ori-learnerspdf-0

Education Review Office. (2016a). *Equity and excellence in student outcomes.* Wellington: Author. Retrieved from https://www.ero.govt.nz/publications/communities-of-learning-kahui-ako-collaboration-to-improve-learner-outcomes/equity-and-excellence-in-student-outcomes

Education Review Office. (2016b). *School leadership that works.* Wellington: Author.

Fullan, M. (2011). *Learning is the work.* Unpublished paper. Retrieved from http://thequohaslostitsstatus.weebly.com/uploads/5/4/2/3/54231535/__learning_is_the_work.pdf

Gibbs, P., & Angelides, P. (2008). Understanding friendship between critical friends. *Improving Schools, 11*(3), 213–225. https://dx.doi.org/10.1177%2F1365480208097002

Glaser, J. E. (2013). *Conversational intelligence: How great leaders build trust and get extraordinary results.* Brookline, MA: Bibliomotion.

Grudnoff, L., Haigh, M., Hill, M. F., Cochran-Smith, M., Ell, F., & Ludlow, L. (2017). Teaching for equity: Insights from international evidence with implications for a teacher education curriculum. *The Curriculum Journal, 28*(3), 305–326. http://dx.doi.org/10.1080/09585176.2017.1292934

Grudnoff, L., Haigh, M., Jackson, C., & Passfield, P. (2018). Using collaborative inquiry to examine equity-linked problems of practice. *Set: Research Information for Teachers, 2*, 33–39. https://doi.org/10.18296/set.0107

Hill, M. F. (2016). Assessment for learning community: Learners, teachers and policymakers. In D. Wyse, L. Hayward, & J. Pandya (Eds.), *The Sage handbook of curriculum, pedagogy and assessment* (Vol. 2, pp. 772–789). London, UK: Sage.

Hynds, A., & McDonald, L. (2010). Motivating teachers to improve learning for culturally diverse students in New Zealand: Promoting Māori and Pacific Islands student achievement. *Professional Development in Education, 36*(3), 525–540. https://doi.org/10.1080/19415250903319275

James, M., & Pollard, A. (2011). TLRP's ten principles for effective pedagogy: Rationale, development, evidence, argument and impact. *Research Papers in Education, 26*(3), 275–328. https://doi.org/10.1080/02671522.2011.590007

Jesson, R., Wilson, A., McNaughton, S., & Lai, M. (2017). *Teachers leading inquiry for school problem solving.* Wellington: NZCER Press.

Lai, M. K., & McNaughton, S. (2008). Raising student achievement in poor communities. In L. M. Earl & H. Timperley (Eds.), *Professional learning conversations: Challenges in using evidence for improvement* (pp. 13–27). London, UK: Springer. https://doi.org/10.1007/978-1-4020-6917-8_2

Lave, J., & Wenger, E. (1991). *Situated learning: Legitimate peripheral participation.* New York, NY: Cambridge University Press.

Matamua, R. (2017*). Matariki: The star of the year.* Wellington: Huia.

MET Project. (2013). *Ensuring fair and reliable measures of effective teaching: Culminating findings from the MET project's three-year study.* Bill and Melinda Gates Foundation. Retrieved from http://k12education.gatesfoundation.org/resource/ensuring-fair-and-reliable-measures-of-effective-teaching-culminating-findings-from-the-met-projects-three-year-study/

Ministry of Education. (2007). *The New Zealand curriculum.* Wellington: Learning Media. Retrieved from www.nzcurriculum.tki.org.nz/The-New-Zealand-Curriculum

Ministry of Education. (2012, January). *The New Zealand Curriculum* Treaty of Waitangi principle. *The New Zealand Curriculum Update,* (16). Retrieved from https://nzcurriculum.tki.org.nz/Curriculum-resources/NZC-Updates/Issue-16-January-2012

Ministry of Education. (2018). *Our schooling futures: Stronger together Whiria ngā kura tūātinitini*. Report by the Tomorrow's Schools Independent Taskforce. Retrieved from https://conversation.education.govt.nz/assets/TSR/Tomorrows-Schools-Review-Report-Dec2018.PDF

Opfer, V. D., & Pedder, D. (2011). Conceptualizing teacher professional learning. *Review of Educational Research, 81*(3), 376–407. https://doi.org/10.3102/0034654311413609

Popp, J., & Goldman, S. (2016, October). Knowledge building in teacher professional learning communities: Focus of meeting matters. *Teaching and Teacher Education, 59*, 347–359. https://doi.org/10.1016/j.tate.2016.06.007

Poskitt, J. (2005). Towards a model of New Zealand school-based teacher professional development. *New Zealand Journal of Teachers' Work, 2*(2), 136–151.

Robinson, V., Hohepa, M., & Lloyd, C. (2009). *School leadership and student outcomes: Identifying what works and why. Best evidence synthesis iteration.* Wellington: Ministry of Education.

Scardamalia, M., & Bereiter, C. (2003). Knowledge building. In J. W. Guthrie (Ed.), *Encyclopedia of education* (2nd ed.). New York, NY: Macmillan Reference.

Sinnema, C., Alansari, M., & Turner, H. (2018). *The promise of improvement through and of the Teacher Led Innovation Fund: Evaluation of the Teacher-Led Innovation Fund: Final report.* Retrieved from: https://www.educationcounts.govt.nz/publications/schooling/evaluation-of-the-teacher-led-innovation-fund-final-report

Snook, I., & O'Neill, J. (2014). Poverty and inequality of educational achievement. In V. Carpenter & S. Osborne (Eds.), *Twelve thousand hours: Education and poverty in Aotearoa New Zealand* (pp. 19–43). Auckland: Dunmore Publishing.

Timperley, H., Kaser, L., & Halbert, J. (2014, April). *A framework for transforming learning in schools: Innovation and the spiral of inquiry.* Seminar Series Paper No. 234. East Melbourne, VIC: Centre for Strategic Education.

Timperley, H., Wilson, A., Barrar, H., & Fung, I. (2007). *Teacher professional learning and development: Best evidence synthesis iteration (BES).* Wellington: Ministry of Education.

# Index

achievement 6, 79
  and ethnicity 1, 2
  gap between high-achieving and low-achieving learners 1
  and socioeconomic class 1, 2
ako 14
Asian students, achievement 1

behaviour management *see* challenging behaviour of students
Best Evidence Synthesis programme (BES: Aotearoa New Zealand) 4–5, 7, 8, 78, 79
Bill and Melinda Gates Foundation 5
buddies, to build communication in mathematics 31–34

"can-do/must-do" strategy 55, 56
capacity building 63–64
challenging behaviour of students 16, 21–22
  analysis of incidents 53–55, 56–57, 59, 76–77
  building independence in learners to increase agency 55–56
  CIT inquiry data collection 52–54, 56–57, 59, 76–77
  impact on learning of other students 51
  increase 51, 52, 55, 56
  increasing motivation and engagement of students 58–59
  triggers 52, 54, 57
child–child communication 31
Cochran-Smith, Marilyn 23, 67, 69–70
collaboration
  problem-solving 32
  student collaboration with their families 43–46

collaborative inquiry communities 9–10, 11
  *see also* Teaching for Equity: How Do We Do It? project
  implications and possibilities from Teaching for Equity: How Do We Do It? project 79–81
  value of cross-sector communities 79
communication
  child–child communication 31
  classroom patterns 31, 34
  digital systems 46–47, 49
  mathematical communication 29, 31–32
  online knowledge sharing vs face-to-face 14–15, 19, 70–71, 80–81
  open communication 18–19
  shared vocabulary 20
  talking past each other 20
  with parents and whānau 40–48, 49–50
communities of learning 48
conceptual development 6
content of curriculum 6, 8, 72, 73
context 8, 11, 14
conversations
  Glaser's conversational intelligence matrix 71
  knowledge-building moves 18–19, 70, 71–72
  professional learning 69, 72, 76
CREDE (Center for Research on Education, Diversity, and Excellence: United States) 7–8
CREDE Five Standards for Effective Pedagogy and Learning 8
critical-friend relationships 16, 58
critical habit of mind 9, 24
critical thinking 7
culture
  diversity 19, 29, 69, 72
  relevance of curriculum content 6

curriculum
  content 6, 8
  *New Zealand Curriculum* 2, 8–9
  school focus area 10

data collection and analysis 16, 20, 22, 24, 38, 52–55, 56–57, 59, 68, 76–77, 80
deputy principals (DPs) 15, 51, 52, 65, 73–74
digital communication systems 46–47, 49
  online knowledge sharing vs face-to-face 14–15, 19, 70–71, 80–81
disability
  impact on opportunities and outcomes 2, 48
  provision for children with special needs 14, 22, 73
diversity
  in collaborative inquiry 17, 19–20, 22, 68, 69, 72–73
  students 7, 14, 22, 29, 59, 69
  teachers 11

Education Review Office (ERO) 2, 61
*Effective Pedagogy in Mathematics* (Anthony & Walshaw, 2007) 5
*Effective Pedagogy in Social Sciences* (Aitken & Sinnema, 2008) 5
electronic portfolios 40, 46–47
engagement
  parents 43
  principals and deputy principals 63, 65, 74
  students 6, 34, 36, 44, 56, 58
  teachers 7, 9, 10, 12, 15, 65, 73, 74, 78, 79, 80, 81
equality, distinguished from equity 2–3, 15, 48–49, 73, 80
equity
  *see also* Facets of Practice for Equity; Teaching for Equity: How Do We Do It? project
  challenging practices that reproduce inequities 8, 14, 21, 51–52, 56, 59–60, 72–73, 79–80
  distinguished from equality 2–3, 15, 48–49, 73, 80
  enhancing through inquiry: key findings 66–81
  teaching to promote 1–2, 3
ethics, practitioner inquiry 16
ethnicity, impact on opportunities and outcomes 1, 2
evidence 7, 10, 14, 17, 22, 25, 69, 80
  evaluation 7
  experiential evidence 24, 25
  Facet 4, *Using evidence to scaffold learning and improve teaching* 7, 30, 31, 37, 72, 78
  sharing with learners 34–37
expertise in collaborative inquiry 22–23, 59, 60, 67, 68–70, 75, 77

face-to-face discussions 14–15, 19, 70–71, 80–81
Facet 2,
  buddies to build communication in mathematics 31–34
  building stronger partnerships with parents and whānau 39–50
Facets of Practice for Equity 3–4, 14
  buddies to build communication in mathematics 31–34
  building stronger partnerships with parents and whānau 39–50
  comparing research and developing facets 6–8, 76
  expanding knowledge of the facets 20–22, 24, 78
  Facet 1, *Selecting worthwhile content and designing and implementing learning opportunities aligned to valued learning outcomes* 6, 72, 73, 78

Facet 2 *Connecting to students as learners, and to their lives and experiences* 6, 8, 21, 30–31, 31–34, 39–40, 72, 75–76, 78

Facet 3, *Creating learning-focused, respectful and supportive learning environments* 7, 72, 78

Facet 4, *Using evidence to scaffold learning and improve teaching* 7, 30, 31, 37, 72, 78

Facet 5, *Adopting an inquiry stance and taking responsibility for further professional engagement and learning* 7–8, 78

Facet 6, *Recognising and seeking to address classroom, school and societal practices that reproduce inequity* 8, 21, 51, 56, 59–60, 72–73, 78

Fairburn School's use in teaching of mathematics inquiries 27–38
identifying and selecting research programmes/syntheses 4–6, 7–8
and teacher inquiry 10–11, 15–16, 17, 24, 48–49, 59–60, 67, 68, 69, 70, 72, 75–76, 77–78

Fairburn School 11
CIT collaborative inquiry with New Lynn School 51–56, 59–60, 62–64, 73–74, 79
CIT investigations into mathematics teaching 27–38
"white stick" incidents of behavioural difficulties 52, 53–56

feedback 7
formative assessment 29, 30
funding for schools 2–3

gender, impact on opportunities and outcomes 2
Glaser's conversational intelligence matrix 71
Google Docs 14, 53

group discussion
project 18–20
students 30, 32, 33, 36

homework
examples of projects 43–45
investigating new approaches 43–46, 47
parent and whānau survey 41–42

inequity *see* equity
initial teacher education
*see also* Project RITE
challenging inequities 3
inquiry *see* research and inquiry
iPad videos 32, 33–34, 35, 36, 37

Ka Hikitia strategy 1
knowledge-building 14–15, 75, 80–81
conversational processes 18–19, 70, 71–72
Knowledge Forum software 14

language
diversity 29, 30, 33
home languages 29, 30, 31, 32, 33
impact on opportunities and outcomes 2
mathematical language 29, 30, 32
relevance of curriculum content 6
language-experience approach to writing 58
leadership in schools and collaborative inquiry 61–62, 65, 73–74

mana 45
manaakitanga 18, 42
Māori
CIC member expertise 69
tuakana–teina relationship 31–32

Māori students
*see also* Te Kotahitanga project
    achievement 1
    BES programme 7
    New Lynn and Fairburn primary schools 11
Matariki 36
mathematics
    discussion and talk in classrooms 29–31, 32–37
    vocabulary 29, 30, 32, 34, 35, 37
mathematics teaching 16
    *Effective Pedagogy in Mathematics* (Anthony & Walshaw, 2007) 5
    Fairburn School inquiries 27–38
    measurement in mathematics 33–34
    "must-do/can-do" strategy 55–56
    sharing evidence with learners 34–37
    using buddies to build communication 31–34
mauri 19
Measures of Effective Teaching project (MET: United States) 5–6, 7, 8
meetings 18, 23, 60, 62–63, 64, 65, 67, 70, 73, 74
    off-site project meetings 48
    online vs face-to-face meetings 14–15, 19, 70–71, 80–81
    parent–teacher meetings 46
metacognitive strategies 7
Ministry of Education 2, 9
moral purpose of changing practice 10–11, 24
motivation
    students 6, 33, 44, 45, 55, 58
    teachers 24, 67, 74, 77
"must-do / can-do" strategy 55, 56

New Lynn School 11
    CIT collaborative inquiry with Fairburn School 51–53, 56–60, 62–64, 73–74, 79
    CIT inquiries into partnerships with parents and whānau 39–50
    incidents of student behavioural difficulties 52–53, 56–57
*New Zealand Curriculum* 2, 8–9

online knowledge sharing vs face-to-face 14–15, 19, 70–71, 80–81

Pākehā students, achievement 1
parents
    collaboration with students 43–46
    engagement with schools 10, 16, 21, 25
    homework survey 41–42
    New Lynn School inquiries into stronger partnerships 39–50
Pasifika Education Plan 1
Pasifika students
    achievement 1
    BES programme 7
    example of a homework project by one student 44–45
    New Lynn and Fairburn primary schools 11
photographs as evidence 36, 37
practitioner research and inquiry xiii, 9, 16, 23–25, 52, 64
principals' perspectives on Teaching for Equity: How Do We Do It? project 61–65, 73, 74
prior knowledge 6, 20–21
problem-solving 31, 32, 34–37
professional learning 7, 9, 10, 48, 69–70
    conversations 69, 72, 76
    mathematics 29
    principals' engagement 65
    viewed as "add-ons" 10
Project RITE 3–4, 7
    *see also* Facets of Practice for Equity

*Quality Teaching for Diverse Students* (Alton-Lee, 2003) 5

reciprocity 18
relational trust 18, 70–71, 79
research and inquiry 8–9
    *see also* collaborative inquiry communities; Teaching and Learning Research Initiative (TLRI) funding; Teaching for Equity: How Do We Do It? project
    cyclical process 9
    different forms of inquiry 23–25, 75–76
    how to research 22
    inquiry as stance 7, 9, 24, 68, 69, 75, 76–77
    practitioner research and inquiry xiii, 9, 16, 23–25, 52, 64
    principals' perspectives on teacher inquiry 64
    relationship between research and practice xii–xiii, 23–24
respect 17, 18, 57, 71
    Facet 3, *Creating learning-focused, respectful and supportive learning environments* 7, 72, 78
Rethinking Initial Teacher Education (RITE) *see* Project RITE

scaffolding 7, 30, 31, 37, 55
schools
    *see also* Fairburn School; New Lynn School; Teaching for Equity: How Do We Do IT? project
    challenging practices that reproduce inequities 8, 14, 21, 51–52, 56, 59–60, 72–73, 79–80
    engagement with family and whānau 10, 16, 19, 21, 25, 39–50
    focus areas 10, 27
    per-student funding 2–3
    school–home connections analysis 40–41

Seesaw e-portfolio system 40, 46–47
self-learning 7
social justice 2, 3, 24, 59
socioeconomic class 22
    impact on opportunities and outcomes 1, 2
special needs 2, 14, 22, 48, 73
students
    *see also* Asian students; challenging behaviour of students; Facet 2, *Connecting to students as learners, and to their lives and experiences*; homework; Māori students; Pākehā students; parents; Pasifika students; schools; whānau
    belonging 7
    building independence in learners to increase agency 55–56
    diversity 7, 14, 22, 29, 59, 69
    engagement 6, 34, 36, 44, 56, 58
    motivation 6, 33, 44, 45, 55, 58
    participation 2, 6, 29, 30–31, 32, 33, 34–35, 36, 37, 44, 56
    teachers' cognitive, social and emotional connections 7

Te Kotahitanga project 7, 8, 78
Teacher-led Innovation Fund (TLIF) 9, 76
Teaching and Learning Research Initiative (TLRI) funding 2, 23, 64, 68, 74, 75
Teaching and Learning Research Programme (TLRP: United Kingdom) 5, 7, 8
Teaching for Equity: How Do We Do It? project 2, 3, 13–17, 25–26, 50, 51
    *see also* Facets of Practice for Equity
    building relationships 17–18, 39–50
    capacity building 63–64
    Collaborative Inquiry Teams (CITs) 15–16, 23, 24, 25, 26, 67, 75–77, 79 (*see also under* Fairburn School; New Lynn School)

data collection and analysis 16, 20, 22, 24, 38, 52–55, 56–57, 59, 68, 76–77, 80
diversity 17, 19–20, 22, 68, 69, 72–73
final report availability 40
implications and possibilities for collaborative enquiry 79–81
key findings 66–81
learning about different forms of inquiry 23–25
meetings 18, 23, 48, 60, 62–63, 64, 65, 67, 70, 73, 74
open communication and sharing of ideas 14–15, 18–19
outsider and insider expertise 22–23, 59, 60, 67, 68–70, 75, 77
principals' perspectives 61–65
resourcing 23, 64, 68, 74–75, 80
university participation and leadership 11, 15, 19, 22–23, 48, 59, 62, 63, 66, 68, 69, 73, 74–75, 76

Tomorrow's Schools Independent Taskforce 9
Treaty of Waitangi 2
trust, in collaborative inquiry 17–18, 60, 65, 67, 70–72, 73, 79, 80, 81
tuakana–teina relationship 31–32, 33–34

university participation and leadership in collaborative inquiries 11, 15, 19, 22–23, 48, 59, 62, 63, 66, 68, 69, 73, 74–75, 76

videos
    iPad videos 32, 33–34, 35, 36, 37
    on Seesaw 47
vulnerability 18, 71

whānau 16, 19, 21, 25
    collaboration with students 43–46
    homework survey 41–42
    New Lynn School inquiries into stronger partnerships 39–50

whanaungatanga 18
"working the dialectic" xii–xiii
writing difficulties 57–59

www.ingramcontent.com/pod-product-compliance
Lightning Source LLC
Chambersburg PA
CBHW080808300426
44114CB00020B/2870